SNAKES·&·LIZARDS

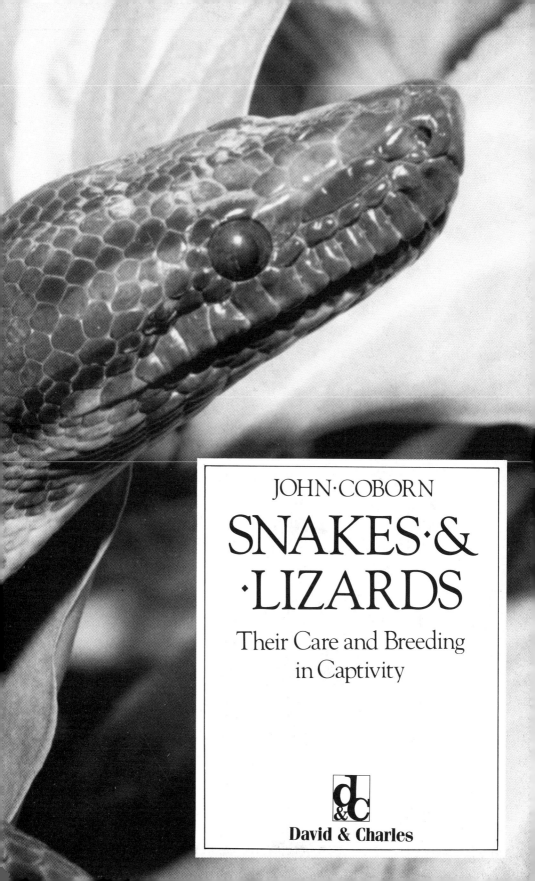

JOHN·COBORN

SNAKES·&
·LIZARDS

Their Care and Breeding
in Captivity

dc
&

David & Charles

(*half-title*) Crocodile lizard, *Shinisaurus crocodilurus*. This semi-aquatic species, from China, is rarely seen in captivity (*Dave Barker, Dallas*) (*Title page, main picture*) One of the most beautiful, docile, and sought after boids is the rainbow boa, *Epicrates cenchria*; (*inset left*) The ever popular green iguana, *Iguana iguana*, is one of the most interesting and endearing terrarium inmates. It is a sad fact that these beautiful creatures are extensively hunted by man, for food, in their native habitat; (*inset right*) Caucasian agama, *Agama caucasia*, requires similar care to that described for *Agama mutabilis* (*B. Langerwerf*)

ERRATUM

Colour Plate 31 shows the Timber Rattlesnake (*Crotalus horridus*) not the Prarie Rattlesnake (*C. viridis*)

British Library Catalouging in Publication Data

Coborn, John
  Snakes & Lizards: their care and breeding
  in captivity.
  1. Lizards as pets   2. Snakes as pets
  I. Title   II. Kelsey-Wood, Dennis
  639.3'96   SF459.L5
  ISBN 0-7153-8814-2

First published 1987
Reprinted 1991

Text and illustrations © John Coborn 1987

Typeset by Photographics, Honiton, Devon
and printed in Great Britain by Redwood Press Ltd, Melksham, Wilts
for David & Charles
Brunel House   Newton Abbot   Devon

CONTENTS

ACKNOWLEDGEMENTS

This book is dedicated to all those colleagues and friends of the author, past and present, who have given him material assistance, moral encouragement or a combination of both in his herpetological career to date; in particular the following:

Claes Andren (Sweden), Nick Arnold (UK), James Ashe (Kenya), Roger Avery (UK), Dave Ball (UK), Robert Baltrock (UK), Chris Banks (Australia), A. Bannikov (USSR), Ibrahim Baran (Turkey), George Barker (UK), Jon Barzdo (UK), Trevor Beebee (UK), Angus Bellairs (UK), Ann Bizony (UK), Quentin Bloxam (Jersey), Hans Boos (Trinidad), Bill Branch (South Africa), Maureen Clifford (UK), Malcolm Coe (UK), John and Margaret Cooper (UK), Keith Corbett (UK), Jack Corney (UK), John Cortes (Gibraltar), Lord Cranbrook (UK), Peter Davies (UK), Dag Dolmen (Norway), Edward Elkan (UK), Paul van den Elzen (South Africa), Mark Ferguson (N. Ireland), John Field (UK), John Foden (UK), Dieter Glandt (German Federal Republic), John Griffin (UK), Kurt Grossenbacher (Switzerland), Eduardo Gudynas (Uruguay), Torkel Hagström (Sweden), Rick Hahn (USA), Keith Harding (UK), Wim Hendrix (Netherlands), John Heyworth (UK), Rene Honegger (Switzerland), Tom Huff (Canada), Barbara Jackson (UK), Oliphant Jackson (UK), Ted Joanen (USA), Dennis and Eve Kelsey-Wood (UK), Walter Kirsche (German Democratic Republic), Konrad Klemmer (German Federal Republic), Mike Lambert (UK), Joseph Laszlo (USA), Keith Lawrence (UK), Nick Millichamp (UK), Desmond Morris (UK), Johnny Morris (UK), Richard and Lisa Needham (UK), Goran Nilsen (Sweden), Tony Phelps (UK), Don Reid (UK), Jenny Remfry (UK), Joan Robb (New Zealand), Richard Ross (USA), Walter Sachsse (German Federal Republic), Loic Sautereau (France), Brian Savage (UK), Julian and Jane Sims (UK), Brian Sinfield (UK), Frank Slavens (USA), Ian Spellerberg (UK), Richard Straton (UK), Anton Stumpel (Netherlands), Mike Sutton (UK), Ian Swingland (UK), Chris Tarrant (UK), Bill Timmis (UK), John Tranter (UK), Wincey Willis (UK).

Illustrations include a number of charming engravings from *The Illustrated Natural History* by the Rev J.G. Wood, MA, FLS, which was first published in 1871 by George Routledge and Sons, London.

The author would also like to express thanks to those people who kindly supplied photographs for inclusion in the work; to Peter Daly for his excellent line drawings and to the Midland Pet Reptilium of Walsall for allowing the author to photograph numerous specimens in their possession. Finally, and most important of all, my wife Ingrid – who has steadfastly supported my herpetological pursuits in spite of the many personal sacrifices this has entailed. Without that support there could have been no book.

John Coborn
Pensilva, Cornwall

INTRODUCTION

Numerous books about reptiles and amphibians, including some on the captive care of these fascinating creatures, have been published. However, many of these are outdated, whilst others attempt to encompass the whole range of newts, salamanders, frogs, toads, turtles, terrapins, tortoises, crocodilians, lizards and snakes in a single volume; a difficult task to accomplish comprehensively.

In this book, the reader is introduced to the lizards and snakes, which comprise the order Squamata of the class Reptilia, and is guided into the science of captive husbandry. With many thousands of species in existence it is clearly almost impossible to cover more than a representative selection of them in a single volume and the author has attempted, with some difficulty, to include those which are more readily available. To these have been added a few which may only be obtained in certain countries (eg Australia) or are unusual enough to warrant special attention. The work is suited both for the beginner and for the more advanced herpetologist and, it is hoped, will also be of interest to the general naturalist. The author hesitates in using the word 'pet' to describe reptiles; anyone requiring such an animal should turn to a cat or dog, rabbit or budgerigar. Lizards and snakes are kept for their aesthetic and scientific interest rather than as members of the family.

While it has been considered necessary to include sections on herpetological history, evolution, classification and general biology, the major part of the work is devoted to the correct husbandry and, in particular, the ultimate breeding of lizards and snakes. It can be safely said that, if an animal successfully reproduces in captivity, optimum conditions have been achieved. This applies particularly to the lower vertebrates, which are unable to adapt to conditions alien to them, and it is only recently that advances in our knowledge of captive propagation in relation to wild habitat have rendered the captive breeding of most reptile species within the reach of the amateur enthusiast. With the increasing pressures on all forms of wild life, particularly with regard to the changes in natural biotopes due to exploitation by man for agricultural, industrial, or residential purposes, it is the duty of every reptile keeper to encourage his charges to reproduce. The ultimate aim should be that it becomes unnecessary to collect wild specimens for the benefit of scientific research, exhibition or for the pet market. Unfortunately, even now,

The author, during the one of his 'Ashmolean Christmas Lectures for Children' in Oxford, England. The children are admiring a boa constrictor (*Oxford and County Newspapers*)

far too many specimens from the wild are 'consumed' by the pet trade, by commercial entrepeneurs using reptile products, and even by some zoological gardens. If this book can help alleviate even a small proportion of these injustices to the world's natural heritages, it will have achieved its purpose.

Although drawing from his own experiences, which have included many aspects of herpetology from collecting and observing reptiles in the field to the keeping of numerous species in captivity, the author could not have produced this work without reference to a considerable amount of literature. A list of useful books, periodicals and important papers is therefore given in the Bibliography for further reading.

1·ATTITUDES, TRADE AND LEGISLATION

Snakes and lizards, in particular the former, bring out a whole range of reactions from man and the maxim 'either you love them or you hate them', can be applied to all reptiles with the possible exception of the turtles and the tortoises, which tend to attract a greater band of admirers than other reptilian orders. The very mention of the word snake in the average household will produce shudders and grimaces of distaste, whilst the sudden appearance of a serpent, however harmless, is enough to strike terror in the hearts of a vast percentage of the world's population. It is perhaps easy to understand this universal loathing of one of God's creatures, whose evil reputation began in the Garden of Eden. In spite of the fact that only ten per cent of the total snake species are venomous, and an even smaller percentage dangerously so, the serpentine form has throughout history been a symbol of fear to the vast majority. There is evidence to suggest that this fear is acquired rather than inherited. Small babies will handle snakes quite fearlessly and it is usually at about the time of puberty that the greatest repulsion begins to manifest itself. This arises from discussion with parents, relatives and friends, who are continually reminding each other that they cannot stand snakes every time the subject arises.

Serpents are often used in the media for sensationalism; they are frequently seen in films, usually as additional creepy material in thrillers; and they grace the jackets of many books. Scientific correctness is rarely a major objective in such exploitations of the reptiles and common harmless snakes usually act as 'stand-ins' for their deadly relatives. It is also not uncommon to see Tarzan wrestling with a boa constrictor or a reticulated python in the African jungle, when the former is native to South America, the latter to south-east Asia.

Snakes have featured in the folklore of many cultures for generations and not always have they played the villainous role. The Greek god of healing, Aesculapius, carried a staff entwined with one or two serpents (depending on the artist) and this staff has become the symbol of many organisations connected with health, hygiene and medicine. The European Aesculapean snake, *Elaphe longissima*, is so named after this apparent association. In Central America, the

Aztecs worshipped Quetzalcoatl, the plumed serpent, as the 'master of life', whilst the Chinese Imperial Dragon is said to be a mixture of lizard, snake and crocodile. Many forms of reptiles appear in primitive cave drawings and lizards and snakes appear on the decorative artifacts of aboriginals. Snakes feature prominently in certain religions, ranging from python worship in parts of Africa and India to the elaborate ceremonies of Christian sects in the southern USA and in Italy. In Malaya, the well known Snake Temple of Penang contains hundreds of snakes, mainly Wagler's pit vipers, *Trimeresurus wagleri*, and is a popular tourist attraction.

The fascination of reptiles has, not surprisingly, produced a number of famous, and infamous characters, the former dedicted scientists with a genuine interest, the latter sensationalists, who perform ego boosting tricks such as wrestling with anacondas or allowing themselves to be bitten by venomous snakes. The word herpetology (derived from the Greek *herpeton* – a creeping thing) describes the study of reptiles and amphibians, assumingly in a scientific manner; the word herpetologist is unfortunately often misapplied. The keeper of a single python in a glass tank can hardly be described as a herpetologist, any more than the owner of a pet budgerigar can be termed an ornithologist.

Zoos, Societies and the Pet Trade

The advent of zoological gardens in the latter half of the nineteenth century aroused a wider interest in exotic reptiles – species hitherto unknown to city dwellers could be viewed through the glass windows of primitive vivaria, most of which were little more than aquarium tanks without water. Needless to say, zoos were initially consumers of reptiles (as well as other animals), and it was always fairly simple to capture or import a new specimen to replace the caged example which had died. Due to a lack of knowledge of basic requirements, reptiles died of starvation, if not from disease, and captive breeding was virtually unheard of. Even as recently as the 1950s, reproduction of reptiles in captivity was the exception rather than the rule, and it is only during the last two or three decades that major advancements in our knowledge of reproductive biology in reptiles has helped alleviate the problem to a certain extent, although further progress is still urgently required.

Although many zoos have taken a sensible scientific approach in the exhibition of reptiles, there still remains an element of sensationalism which, many will argue, is a necessity in order to induce the public to part with valuable entrance money. The author himself pleads guilty to such a project when, as director of a zoological garden, he organised a snake 'sit-in', in which a young South African lived for seventy-three days in a specially constructed cage with two dozen assorted venomous snakes, ranging from Indian cobras to puff adders, and thus breaking the unofficial world record for such a feat. The motive, of course, was to boost zoo funds through the publicity afforded. It is surely a sad fact that such tactics often have to be resorted to in order to keep some zoos viable.

It is difficult to make a strong division between what is morally right or wrong in publicising herpetology, although it is a fairly obvious fact that certain aspects of sensationalism have performed a service to the science by arousing the interests of people who may never have become the eminent professional herpetologists or learned amateurs that they are. One of the most famous herpetologists of the century, and one who has influenced many others, both in person and through his writings, was Raymond L. Ditmars (1876–1942), for many years Curator of Reptiles at the Bronx Zoos in New York. In 1907 his work *The Reptile Book* was published and this rapidly became the bible for contemporary herpetologists. Further publications by Ditmars, including *Snakes of the World* (1931) and *Reptiles of the World* (1933), although outdated by today's standards, remain classics of herpetological literature. It was Ditmars who led the field in publicity when it came to promoting his subject; being a former newspaper reporter, the press was summoned at every opportunity. Whether to force feed a python or to milk a venomous snake, his techniques have been followed by generations of herpetologists.

It was after World War II that the major interest in herpetology developed and groups of interested individuals soon got together to form societies dedicated to the study of herptiles (a convenient term which collectively describes amphibians and reptiles) and the furtherance of all aspects of herpetological science, ranging from field observation to captive husbandry and breeding. The leaders of the field were the USA, Great Britain and Germany which, collectively, can probably still boast by far the greatest majority of amateur and professional herpetologists in the world. Other countries have followed, and today there is a healthy international interest in this hitherto maligned group of vertebrates. Not surprisingly, disputes have frequently arisen between the conservationist and pet-keeping lobbies, the former maintaining that the collection of wild specimens for the pet-trade can never be justified, the latter arguing that many species may be lost forever unless a successful captive breeding programme is instigated.

In the last decade a new phenomenon has arisen in the form of herpetological symposia, in which both amateur and professional herpetologists get together in order to share information through the reading of papers and to discuss points of mutual interest. One of

Sail-finned lizard, *Hydrosaurus pustulatus*. A semi-aquatic species from the East Indies. Requires similar care to that of the water dragon, *Physignathus cocincinus* (*Dave Barker, Dallas*)

the first such symposia in the United Kingdom was organised by the author in 1975. Entitled 'Conservation and Captive Reptiles and Amphibians', the case for and against captivity as an aid to the preservation of wild species was presented by many herpetologists who expressed their particular views. The success of this first meeting was reflected in the controversial arguments which ensued, but it was evident that the most sensible course lay in greater co-operation between societies and individuals. Further symposia followed annually and in 1980 a European Herpetological Symposium was convened in which herpetologists from throughout Europe presented mainly conservation biased papers at the University of Oxford. This was the first international meeting in which participants came from most West European countries as well as some Eastern bloc states and was universally acclaimed as an unqualified success. The series of symposia culminated in 1981 with the organization of the first International Herpetological Congress, attended by herpetologists from many parts of the world.

Running parallel to these UK symposia were certain meetings organized by the SSAR (Society for the Study of Amphibians and Reptiles) in the USA and by the DGHT (Deutsche Gesellschaft für Herpetologie und Terrarienkunde) in Germany. In 1976 the first annual reptile symposium on Captive Propagation and Husbandry was convened at Frederick, Maryland, USA, as the result of an initiative from a number of zoos, institutions and individuals. These symposia have become highly successful and the proceedings of each and every one contain valuable reference material for herpetologists at all levels.

The rise in interest in captive reptiles produced a new generation of collectors and dealers, particularly during the 1960s when millions of tropical specimens were imported into North America and Europe, a huge percentage dying during transit or within two or three weeks of arrival at their destination. This, of course, was due to the unscrupulous actions of certain individuals who were motivated solely by the prospect of a quick profit, with no regard to the welfare of the animals. Wild collected specimens would go through several hands before reaching their final destinations and the author has been appalled by methods used in the transport and handling of reptiles (as well as other wildlife species), though fortunately these methods are now becoming a thing of the past in most countries. Briefly, the system worked as follows: regional collectors would capture numbers of reptiles, smaller specimens being placed in whatever containers were available, larger ones being restrained by tying the limbs and jaws with twine before delivering them to a regional dealer who would, all too often, keep them unfed in overcrowded conditions until the quantity warranted a trip to the nearest exporting town— sometimes hundreds of miles away. There, the exporter would keep them for a further period in appalling conditions, awaiting orders from the wholesalers in the importing countries. Again, the animals would be packed in overcrowded conditions, sometimes bagged, sometimes not, in bamboo, timber or cardboard crates before being placed in the cargo compartment of a plane, which is normally unheated, to be whisked off to an alien climate—often the winter of a temperate region. Even on arrival at the host country airport, respite was rarely immediately forthcoming; crates could lay for hours in the corner of some unheated cargo warehouse whilst the importer haggled over some petty restriction in order to achieve customs clearance.

Eventually the animals arrived at the distributors, where at least some effort would be made to save the lives of those which were not already too far gone. The ordeal was still far from over, however, the reptiles having to be shipped to the wholesalers and the retailers, many of which had little more than a monetary interest in them. At last, the poor creatures reached the purchaser, more often than not in a disease ridden, emaciated, half-starved and chilled condition, having spent up to six months from the point of capture to the living-room vivarium.

Legislation
In recent years, the efforts of conservationists have vastly improved the fate of many species. Some countries have introduced a total ban

on the export of native amphibians and reptiles, others on selected endangered species. In 1973 the *Convention on International Trade in Endangered Species of Flora and Fauna* (CITES), which is sometimes referred to as the 'Washington Convention', heralded the beginnings of a new era in protective legislation. Most countries have ratified the convention or incorporated it in part or in whole with national legislation. Species are categorised depending on their wild status; Appendix I, listing those types regarded as threatened and Appendix II, those which are likely to become threatened. It is still possible to obtain certain of these animals legally by obtaining permits from the appropriate importing and exporting countries, but there are strict regulations appertaining to the capture, restraint, husbandry and transport of specimens. Certain exceptions may be made with regard to captive bred animals, but all herpetologists are advised to familiarise themselves with the relevant legislation before entering into any deals.

The *Convention on the Conservation of European Wildlife and Natural Habitats*, often referred to as the Berne Convention, is concerned with the protection of many species. In Appendix II, a number of amphibians and reptiles are classed as strictly protected and include thirteen lizard and eleven snake species. All other species of amphibian and reptile are classed as protected in Appendix III.

The helmeted iguana, *Corytophanes cristatus*, is a bizarre tree dweller from Central America, requiring similar care to the anoles

Most countries now have their own laws relating to the capture and keeping of wild animals, including lizards and snakes. In Britain there are several laws with which the prospective snake or lizard keeper should become familiar. Under the *Cruelty to Animals Act* (1878), it is illegal to carry out experiments on any living invertebrates other than under licence from the Home Office. The *Pet Animals Act* (1951) makes it illegal to sell animals except from premises registered for that purpose by the local authority; it may involve the inspection of proposed premises by an appointed officer (usually a veterinarian) to ensure that the accommodation meets all requirements appertaining to the humane treatment of the animals. Animals which are sold by a bona fide breeder are usually exempt from this law.

The *Dangerous Wild Animals Act* (1976) was brought about to protect innocent people from dangerous animals kept by irresponsible persons, and forbids the keeping of a number of listed species except under licence from the local authority. The lizards and snakes involved include the Helodermatidae (gila monster and beaded lizard), the Elapidae (eg cobras, mambas, coral snakes, all Australian venomous snakes) and the Viperidae (vipers and rattlesnakes). Certain colubrid snakes, notably the boomslang, *Dispholidus typus,* and the bird snake, *Thelotornis kirtlandi*, have recently been added to the list. Before a licence is issued an officer appointed by the authority (usually a veterinarian), will inspect the premises and the prospective accommodation for the animals, to ensure that they will be kept in humane conditions and that adequate safety arrangements have been made. Only persons aged eighteen years or over are eligible for a licence, and the applicant is expected to pay a fee for the inspection and the licence, as well as to take out insurance against damage by the animals to persons or property. There has been a remarkable range of attitudes from different local authorities to this legislation and licence fees can vary greatly from area to area. The cost of an insurance policy also seems to have some bearing on whether the issuing officer is a herpetologist or snake hater! The cost involved has certainly made some potential keepers of venomous reptiles think twice before applying for a licence. Zoos, circuses, pet shops and premises registered for experimentation on animals are exempt, but are covered by other legislation.

The *Zoo Licencing Act* (1981) makes it illegal to operate a zoo without first obtaining a licence from the local authority. A zoo can be termed as any premises where live wild animals are exhibited to the public. Before issuing a licence the authority will consider reports submitted by appointed zoo inspectors who will remark on the suitability of the premises and the qualifications of the prospective zoo operator.

In the *Wildlife and Countryside Act* (1981), which annuls the *Conservation of Wild Creatures and Wild Plants Act* (1975), total protection is given to a number of British species including the sand lizard, *Lacerta agilis*, and the smooth snake, *Coronella austriaca*. In addition, the sale or the advertising for sale of all native amphibians and reptiles is forbidden, except under licence. Under the act it is also forbidden to release or allow to escape into the wild, any non-native species.

In the USA, legislation is complicated by the number of different state and city laws plus local bye laws which may impose a total ban on the keeping of reptiles (particularly native species), may allow the keeping of some species only, or allow the keeping of any species. Certain Federal Laws operate on a national basis and are enforced by the United States Fish and Wildlife Service. Such laws are usually concerned with the protection of local endangered species. Prospective lizard or snake keepers in the USA are urged to familiarise themselves with all Federal and local legislation appertaining to the hobby before taking steps to obtain specimens.

In Australia, the *Wildlife Protection (Regulation of Exports and Imports) Act* (1982) enables the country to meet commitments under CITES and complements other Commonwealth and state legislation protecting wildlife by imposing restrictions on international trade in endangered species. The exportation and importation of all live reptiles requires a permit under the Act. The exportation of live Australian reptiles may be permitted only if the proposed export is an inter-zoological gardens transfer between approved zoos; or is for the purpose of prescribed scientific research; or involves a household pet being exported by the owner who is permanently departing from Australia. As in the USA, local legislation varies from state to state (or territory) and the appropriate department of each state should be approached to find out the current situation. Native amphibians and reptiles can be kept legally in most states although the regulations and species differ, but people can usually keep the commoner species without a permit.

The legislation regarding the conservation of reptiles varies considerably from country to country and often depends on the current governments' attitude to wildlife in general. Unstable countries have little or no legislation and may be used as staging posts by smugglers of wildlife from other countries. The situation is complex but interesting, and deserves special study, but space does not permit further discussion here. Information may be obtained from appropriate government bodies, local authorities, conservational organisations or herpetological societies. Useful addresses will be found in the Appendix.

Education and Science

Many of the lower vertebrates, including lizards and snakes, have an important educational significance and the author has seen many examples, particularly in primary schools, of how a vivarium containing such creatures can help revolutionise the teaching of almost any subject. Snakes in particular will rouse a permanent interest in small children if used in a sensible manner, and can be related to biology, geography, history and folklore, mathematics, chemistry, physics, art and almost anything else one may care to think about. A particular case recalled by the author is that in which a class of eight-year-olds took turns in being the snake or the lizard keeper for a week, proudly wearing a badge to that effect.

Reptiles have played their part in scientific study; our knowledge of evolution would be sparse without being able to study modern living specimens. In zoology, reptiles have been popular subjects for biological studies both in the wild and in captivity; the many and varied species of lizards and snakes providing a wealth of interesting materials. Ecology, reproductive biology, genetics, nutrition, regeneration, parthenogenesis, medicine, anatomy and physiology are just some of the subjects offered by reptiles in man's quest for knowledge. Certain reptiles breed readily in laboratory conditions and may be kept for various experiments; embryological studies in particular can provide valuable information in regard to the anatomical and physiological development of the higher vertebrates, including ourselves. Venomous snakes are kept in some institutions for the express purpose of maintaining a steady supply of venom, used to produce antivenenes for the treatment of snakebite. Certain snake venoms are being researched with a view to manufacturing drugs from them, which can be used to treat diseases and conditions in humans. The anti-coagulant effect of the constituents of some venoms has resulted in the production of certain drugs invaluable in the treatment of thrombosis and other related conditions.

The preceding notes are intended to introduce the reader to basic aspects of herpetology and the author does not pretend to have scratched more than the surface of some of the subjects discussed. However, many of these deserve further study, indeed, some herpetologists specialise in one or more peripheral areas and thus perform an additional service to the science.

2·LIZARDS, AMPHISBAENIANS AND SNAKES

The living lizards and snakes of the world form the order Squamata and share the vertebrate (backboned) class Reptilia with three other orders: Chelonia (tortoises, turtles and terrapins); Crocodylia (crocodiles, alligators and the gavial) and Rhynchocephalia (the lizardlike tuatara of New Zealand, comprising just a single species). The biological differences between lizards and snakes are not considered sufficient to warrant a separate order, but are placed respectively in the suborders Lacertilia (sometimes referred to as Sauria), and Serpentes (sometimes referred to as Ophidia). The wormlike, burrowing amphisbaenians are sometimes classed within the Lacertilia and sometimes, as in this book, within their own suborder — Amphisbaenia.

Squamata is by far the largest reptilian order, with approximately 6,000 species, comprising around 3,000 lizards, a similar number of snakes and about 100 amphisbaenians. It is never possible to give exact numbers of living species due to the frequent reclassification by zoologists and the constant possibility of the discovery of new forms, or the extinction of existing ones. By comparison, the other orders of living reptilians are relatively sparse in species numbers; Chelonia with about 200 species, Crocodylia with about 21 and Rhynchocephalia with a single species.

Evolution
In order to understand the position of modern lizards and snakes in zoological classification, it is necessary to briefly discuss their evolution in relation to both the other reptilian orders and other vertebrate classes. It is a well documented fact, backed up by the study of fossils, that all forms of life on this earth originated in the water, and it was during the Devonian period, some 380 million years ago, that the first lobe-finned fishes started to creep out onto the land. These fishes (*Eusthenopteron*) had already developed primitive lungs and strong, leglike fins, which enabled them to crawl over land from one water course to another.

Thirty-five million years later, the first actual amphibian appeared; although still somewhat fishlike in appearance, its fins had developed into four sturdy limbs, each possessing five digits. This animal, which is known as *Ichthyostega*, had a much higher developed sense of smell than its aquatic cousins and thus a longer snout, which enabled it to detect the weaker atmospheric scent of its terrestrial prey.

The Devonian was followed by the Carboniferous period and this was the time that really allowed the development of many species of amphibia — extensive swamps were commonplace over much of the globe, and mud, decaying vegetation and fallen trees provided a perfect environment. Many of the amphibia spent more and more time on land, benefiting from the myriad of invertebrates which had also become terrestrial, eventually only returning to the water in order to spawn and lay their soft eggs which hatched into gill-breathing, fishlike larvae. These developed into land dwelling forms only after a protracted aquatic youth, much like most of our modern amphibia.

Why the land was colonised by these creatures at that particular time is inexplicable, but when one considers that every niche capable of supporting life on this earth has been colonised at some stage, it is not surprising. Even when one niche is destroyed, another one is left to be colonised by something else. That of the amphibian was, however, somewhat limited. Although they could live for long periods on dry land, they had to remain in humid areas and could not go for very long without water as, in dry conditions, fluid loss was rapid through the naked, porous skin.

In order to exploit the land even further, some of the more adventurous amphibia had to develop a means of combating water loss. The answer was a protective cover to the skin, which eventually evolved into the typical reptilian scales. At the same time, the development of the first hard-shelled eggs took place; probably one of the most important single events to higher life on this planet. It meant that internal fertilisation became necessary and that these particular animals were no longer amphibia, but had become primitive, true reptiles which could live and reproduce on land, even considerable distances away from water. Moreover, the eggs could be safely hidden away from predators on dry land; they could be buried under the ground or concealed somewhere amongst dense vegetation. The first eggs were large-yolked, allowing the embryos to develop somewhat further than the larval amphibians and thus stand a better chance of survival. Of course, the embryos still had to go through the early stages of development, but they were now enclosed in a sort of sac called the amniotic membrane. The embryo grew in the waterlike fluid contained in the inner membrane, receiving oxygen from the outside and disposing of carbon dioxide by a means of a further membrane — the allantois. Yet another membrane, called the chorion, surrounded the whole lot just inside the outer shell. The

reptiles had a tremendous advantage over the amphibia which had
to spend all their time near water and lay their eggs in it. The
chances of many of these amphibian eggs, or successive larvae,
eventually reaching maturity were few, as many fish, and all
amphibia, were carnivorous — the larger devouring the smaller, and
the smaller eating the eggs and larvae of the larger, as well as each
other!

Thus the first vertebrates began to colonise the dry land which
had hitherto been the kingdom of plants and some invertebrates.
These reptiles continued to develop into different forms; some
developed their dry land hunting prowess, growing strong muscular
limbs which helped them run fast after prey as well as escape from
larger predators which were also developing. Others returned to the
water to catch fish or amphibia in their strong jaws.

At the end of the Carboniferous period, the earth's climate changed
dramatically, many of the typical swamps of the era dried up and

Probable evolutionary lineage of the modern Reptilia. The dotted lines indicate
incomplete fossil evidence. The numbers next to the geological periods on the left
indicate their time scales in millions of years

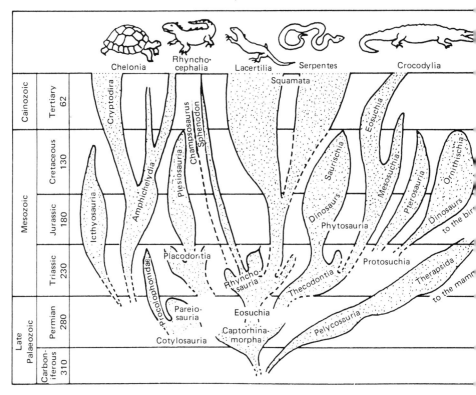

the indigenous amphibia became extinct. This was an advantageous period for the animals which had already begun to colonise the land and which laid shelled eggs. No herbivores had yet developed during the early Permian (280–260 million years ago) and the reptiles had to feed on each other. Various adaptations for gripping, tearing and chewing had to develop in a tremendously competitive time as thousands of different species evolved. Beasts such as *Dimetrodon* had huge sail-like appendages on their backs, just like a solar panel, to help them control their inner temperatures. The sail would be held at right angles to the sun during cool periods and gain maximum benefit from the heat. In case of excessive warmth, the animal would turn so that only the edge of the sail was facing the sun.

Legs grew longer and moved under the body rather than being at the side, thus animals could run faster and for longer. Herbivores developed and most niches were soon taken up by these para-mammals, some of which were believed to have developed fur. In fact, at this time, the first true mammals appeared; those which suckle their young. The next period saw the rise of the dinosaurs, which meant the end of the para-mammals, as the giant reptiles were the dominant animals on earth for the next 140 million years. The only mammals which survived were small nocturnal creatures which were the ancestors of all modern mammals including ourselves.

During the Triassic period (240–200 million years ago), the age of the dinosaurs, some reptiles again took to water, although they continued to lay their eggs on land. One of these, *Proterosuchus*, was similar in appearance to our modern crocodilians and was one of their main ancestors. At the same time, the rhynchocephalians developed several species, the last surviving member of which is the tuatara, *Sphenodon punctatus*, of New Zealand. The Chelonia probably developed a little earlier and are classed as the most primitive of the living reptiles. It is likely that they arose from the cotylosaurs, such as *Limnoscelis*, during the Permian period.

In this era, the ancestors of our modern lizards and snakes were making an appearance, although fossil records of the Squamata are somewhat sparse. The Lacertilia probably branched off from the primitive order Eosuchia during the Triassic period, though the oldest ancestors of our modern lizards are known from fossils of the Upper Jurassic period, about 140 million years ago. The first fossilised bird ancestors are from the same period. Small lizards and snakes, particularly the latter, pose immense problems in palaeonotological study and, unlike the generally massive bones of the dinosaurs, are known only from minute fragments of skull and vertebrae which were scattered far and wide. Piecing such fragments together is infinitely more difficult than the hardest of jig-saw puzzles,

The tuatara, *Sphenodon punctatus*, superficially resembles a lizard, but certain primitive characteristics place it in a separate order (*B. Langerwerf*)

especially when many of the key pieces are missing. Much of our knowledge on the evolution of the order Squamata remains, for the time being, necessarily sparse, but as research continues with modern equipment, we will doubtless soon be able to apply a more positive answer to those questions which remain only partially answered.

It is generally accepted that snakes evolved from the lizards, but no direct connection has yet been discovered. The term 'missing link' is of particular significance when applied to snake evolution; only very small numbers of fossil snake genera have been found and no intermediate species have been discovered. One theory about snakes is that they evolved from burrowing lizards, which first lost their limbs, outer ears and almost their eyesight, the eyes becoming merely vestigial. During the burrowing period, the unique sense of prey detection, using the forked tongue, and possibly the beginnings of heat recepting pits in some species, began to develop. Eventually, certain species again ventured onto the land surface, the lidless eyes redeveloped but external ears and limbs were lost forever, being replaced by other sophisticated means of 'hearing' and locomotion. All this, of course, would have taken millions of years and a corresponding number of generations. Today we still have burrowing snakes, we have the legless amphisbaenians — which possess characteristics of both lizards and snakes, and we have the legless lizards; what we do not have is a concrete link between the suborders. So, for the time being at least, snake evolution still remains a partial mystery.

Classification

As scientists began to catalogue the apparently infinite number of living things it became essential to have some system of classification which was not only logical but also international. Generations of learned people had already been using classical Latin or Greek as a means of communication and it was therefore not surprising that, at the latter part of the eighteenth century, Carl Linnaeus, the father of natural classification, devised his system using these languages as a basis. The pioneer system was, of course, primitive by today's standards but it set a precedent for the following generations of taxonomists.

Natural classification is a hierarchal arrangement of animals or plants into different groups, based on differences and similarities between them. The bottom rank in this arrangement is the species, one of a group of organisms which are all essentially the same, at least with very little variation, and which interbreed to produce more individuals of similar type. A number of species which are not essentially similar, but have several characteristics in common are grouped into a genus (plural genera). Numbers of genera are grouped into families, then into orders, classes and finally into phyla (plural of phylum). The plant equivalent of an animal phylum is a division. The number of similarities between members of a group becomes fewer at each step up the hierarchal ladder, for instance members of the same family have less in common than members of the same genus. In extreme or difficult cases, additional groups such as subfamily or infraorder are used.

The Classification of Reptiles

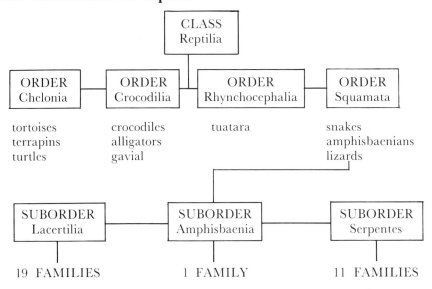

Taxonomy, the study of the theory, procedure and rules of classification of organisms, is a complex subject, and one which has for generations caused much argument and controversy amongst scientists. There have been several schools of thought as to what actually constitutes a natural classification. Some maintain that evolutionary (phylogenetic) relationships should be reflected in classification and assume that members of the same group, at whatever hierarchical level, should share a common ancestry. Taking our knowledge of snake evolution as an extreme example, it can be seen that such a classification is difficult to produce and must be largely based on theory. The procedure of evolution at different rates in different lineages adds a further difficulty to the system. Another theory is that classification should be based on similarities and differences of appearance (phenotype) and include observations on the anatomy, physiology, embryology, cytology and biochemistry of living organisms. Modern classification is based on phylogeny as far as this is known, but in those groups where evolutionary information is sparse then it is supplemented with a degree of calculated guess-work.

The binomial system of nomenclature devised by Linnaeus is still used today, albeit in a much improved form. Each new species is given a two-part name, known as a binomial, made up of the generic name and the specific or trivial name, by the person who first describes it. Thus, in the species *Varanus niloticus* (Nile monitor), *Varanus* is the generic name which is applied to all monitors in that genus, and *niloticus* is the specific name which is applied to a single species only. The name of the discoverer is written after the binomial, for instance the adder, or northern viper, is *Vipera berus* Linnaeus. In addition, the year of description may also be added; thus the rough-scaled bush viper is *Atheris hispidus* Laurent 1955. For general purposes, however, the binomial alone is considered sufficient for normal use.

There are strict rules governing the naming and publishing of new animal species, and these are governed by the International Code of Zoological Nomenclature. An international committee sits at regular intervals to decide whether a new species has been correctly named and to consider proposals for the changing of existing names brought about by reclassification.

Sometimes a third name will be added to the binomial, this being a subspecific name, thus forming a trinomial. This is used when geographical groups of certain species show certain differences, but not enough to warrant classification as a separate species. Subspecies will quite happily interbreed and indeed do so at the borders of their ranges, producing examples with characteristics from both groups; such individuals are known as intergrades. A good example of subspecific nomenclature is that applied to the Indian python, *Python molurus*. When it was decided that the eastern race of this species was sufficiently different to warrant subspecific classification, the subspecies was named *Python molurus bivittatus* (the dark-phase Indian or Burmese python) and the original type-species had the trivial name repeated thus: *Python molorus molorus* (the light-phase Indian python).

Binomials should invariably be written in italic script to avoid confusion with common names or the text in which they are cited and, if it is necessary to use the same name several times in a text, abbreviations may be used as long as the first reference to a particular species is written out in full. For example, the king snake, *Lampropeltis getulus getulus*, may be abbreviated to *L. g. getulus*. Subspecies, such as the Florida and Californian Kings may be abbreviated to *L. g. floridana*, *L. g. californiae* and so on.

Having discussed classification and nomenclature in brief, as applied to the whole of the animal kingdom, but using snakes and lizards as examples, the following table demonstrates the classification of the two species within the order Squamata.

Sample Classification of one Lizard and one Snake

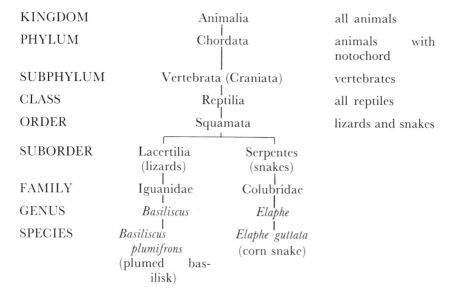

KINGDOM	Animalia		all animals
PHYLUM	Chordata		animals with notochord
SUBPHYLUM	Vertebrata (Craniata)		vertebrates
CLASS	Reptilia		all reptiles
ORDER	Squamata		lizards and snakes
SUBORDER	Lacertilia (lizards)	Serpentes (snakes)	
FAMILY	Iguanidae	Colubridae	
GENUS	*Basiliscus*	*Elaphe*	
SPECIES	*Basiliscus plumifrons* (plumed basilisk)	*Elaphe guttata* (corn snake)	

General Biology

A basic knowledge of reptilian biology is essential for anyone contemplating the keeping of lizards or snakes in the home. All reptiles have certain similarities of form and habit, and an understanding of these will enable herpetoculturists to deal adequately with the animals in their care. As we have seen in the section on evolution, reptiles were the first vertebrates to become fully terrestrial — not needing to return to the water to breed due to the development of the cleidoic egg. Internal fertilisation through copulation, and the cleidoic egg, together constitute one of the great evolutionary advances; without it we humans would not be here today. Of course, the egg alone did not prepare the reptiles for terrestrial habitation, indeed the egg was one of the last adaptations to take place. The whole animal gradually developed characteristics suited to its dry-land life, many of which have been inherited by the living reptiles of today.

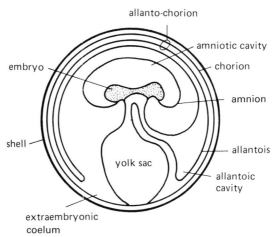

Diagram showing the extraembryonic membranes in the cleidoic egg

Superficially, a reptile is a tetrapod having a skin covered with horny scales, in some species reinforced with bony osteoderms. The skin is relatively waterproof and prevents loss of body fluids through evaporation as well as dilution of the body fluids by osmosis in wet conditions. The head is usually carried on a fairly long neck, and, through articulation of the atlas vertebra with the condyle of the skull, is able to perform the useful function of moving the head from side to side, or up and down. The relatively small brain is encased in a solid bony skull and has a moderately developed cerebrum. A secondary palate, which in the higher vertebrates separates the nasal from the oral cavity, partially occurs in most reptiles; in the croco-dilians it is complete.

The lower jaw consists of three to six separate bones, plus the quadrate which allows articulation with the upper jaw. Teeth are present on the edges of the jaws and, in some species, on the bones of the palate. The teeth may be of several different forms; fused to the sides of the jaws (pleurodont), fused to the summit of the jaws (acrodont), or socketed (thecodont). In most species the teeth are replaced several times in succession (polyphyodont). All species possess a tongue, which may be highly mobile and considerably extensible. The auditory bone (stapes) is single, and a superficial eardrum may be present. The differentiation of the vertebral column into clear cut regions, typical of the mammals, makes its appearance in the reptiles, although it is only the crocodiles which exhibit five distinct regions. The legs are laterally orientated in many species and typically end with five clawed digits. The limbs may be partially reduced or absent in some lizards and invariably absent in snakes.

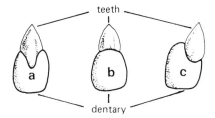

Reptilian dentition: various means by which the teeth are mounted in, or on, the jaw: a) thecodont; b) acrodont; c) pleurodont

All reptiles respire by the means of lungs, and the heart is three chambered (four chambered in the crocodilians). Like the amphibians and fish, reptiles are ectothermic (body heat dependent on environmental temperature), as opposed to the birds and the mammals which are endothermic (body temperature regulated from within).

Due to the immense variety of reptiles amongst the 6,000 or so species, it is difficult to give concise guidelines to their biology and the foregoing serves only as a brief introduction to general anatomy which applies to all reptiles. The order Squamata, however, represents highly specialised groups which have colonised almost every available habitat with the exception of the polar regions. They are found in the arid deserts, the tropical rain forests, the seas, fresh water, alpine meadows, temperate heathland, coniferous forest, and so on. Within these regions they have further adapted to be tree dwelling, terrestrial, burrowing or aquatic. It is little wonder that such a cosmopolitan group has evolved an almost confusing diversity of form. Only the fact that they are ectothermic has prevented them from colonising latitudes and altitudes where the permafrost precludes hibernation below ground.

Biology of Lizards

The most obvious difference between a lizard and a snake is the possession of four well developed limbs in the former, and the total absence of them in the latter. However, there are several lizard

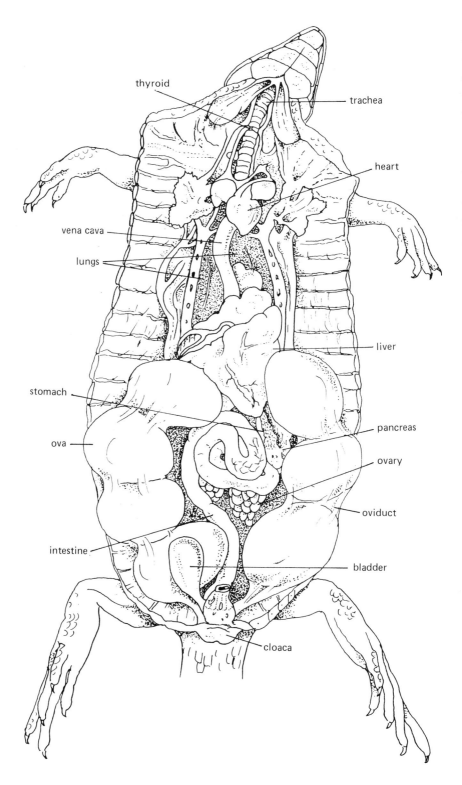

The internal anatomy of a typical female lizard, with the major organs indicated

The rhinoceros iguana, *Cyclura cornuta*, is a large, robust ground lizard from the island of Hispaniola

genera which are superficially legless, others with reduced legs, or a pair of fore or rear limbs only — though vestiges of the pectoral and pelvic girdles may be found in the skeleton. Another difference is the lizard's possession of movable eyelids, but even this is not exclusive as most of the typical geckos, and some skinks, have the snake attribute of fused eyelids, forming a transparent spectacle or brill. In such cases the nictitating membrane, or 'third eyelid', found in all other lizards, is absent. The presence of an external ear opening in the lizards is the third major difference, and is one of the most satisfactory methods of distinguishing a legless lizard from a snake; most lizards have ear openings, snakes do not. Other, less obvious distinguishing features mainly concern internal anatomy. The bones of the lower jaw of lizards are firmly united at the chin whereas in snakes they are joined by elastic tissue; the palatal bones are fixed, unlike those of snakes which are movable — enabling them to swallow larger prey. The teeth of lizards vary in form depending on diet.

The vertebrae of lizards are less articulate than snakes and, in most species, they lack the accessory articulating facets, though some forms show varying stages of development. Locomotion in most species involves lateral movements of the body together with limb movement. All lizards possess a pair of lungs, unlike the snakes which have one functional lung, the other being vestigeal or absent. Many lizard species practise autotomy of the tail as a means of defence. In some species the tail will break off and wriggle violently on being seized by a predator, thus allowing the lizard to escape; a few species are capable of spontaneous autotomy in which the tail is literally thrown off at the approach of great danger. Regeneration of the tail will follow, although secondary tails are generally shorter and less elegant than the original.

Lizards, if anything, show a greater range of adaptation to various modes of life than snakes, and come in a variety of forms ranging from the typical to the bizarre. Size ranges from tiny gekkonids 3cm (1in) in length to giant varanids of 3m (10ft) or more. Size and form may vary greatly, even in individual families; amongst the Varanidae for example, the Australian dwarf monitor, *Varanus brevicauda*, at little more than 20cm (7¾in) total length, compares nicely with the 3.5m (11ft) Komodo dragon, *Varanus komodoensis*, which is the world's largest lizard. The greatest diversity of form in single families is probably demonstrated in the Iguanidae and the Agamidae; the former exhibiting such species as the desert dwelling horned toads, *Phrynosoma cornutum*, with their spiny scales and ant eating habit; the graceful, tree dwelling, herbivorous green iguana, *Iguana iguana*, of the tropical rain forests; the strange, sea-weed eating marine iguana, *Amblyrhynchus cristatus* of the Galapagos Islands; and the large, lumbering rhinoceros iguana, *Cyclura cornuta*, a ground dweller from Haiti. A selection of agamids shows a similar variety; compare the fierce looking, Australian frilled lizard, *Chlamydosaurus kingi* with the green water dragon, *Physignathus cocincinus* of south-east Asia, or the flying lizard, *Draco volans* of Malaysia.

Biology of Amphisbaenians

The wormlike, burrowing amphisbaenians (the name coming from the Greek, meaning 'to move in either direction', doubtless referring to the reptile's ability to move backwards or forwards in its burrow with equal ease) have long been a puzzle to taxonomists. Originally placed within the suborder Lacertilia, they were thought to be a possible link between the lizards and the snakes. However, they show many unique adaptations possessed by neither of these two groups and Amphisbaenia is now generally accepted as an intermediate suborder between the Lacertilia and the Serpentes.

With the exception of the genus *Bipes*, which possesses short forelimbs, the amphisbaenians are limbless, though vestigeal girdles·are present. The tail is usually short and blunt, which has led to a belief amongst some natives that there is a head at each end. The scales are arranged to form girdles around the body, giving an impression of segments as seen in the earthworm. The skull is well ossified, hard and coupled with the broad, shovel-like snout, well adapted for burrowing. The eyes are poorly developed but externally visible. There is no visible ear but the auditory stapes is well developed and useful in picking up vibrations from the substrate. Unlike snakes, the rami of the lower jaw are firmly fused and the tongue cannot be

Frilled lizard, *Chamydosaurus kingi*

Flying lizards, *Draco* species

withdrawn into a sheath. The teeth are usually few in number and may be acrodont or pleurodont. The bones of the palate are rigid and there are no palatal teeth.

Like most lizard species, the vertebrae lack accessory articulating facets. Some species practise caudal autotomy but regeneration is usually incomplete. Unlike the snakes and some lizards, in which the left lung is reduced, amphisbaenians show reduction of the right lung.

Little is known about the breeding biology of the amphisbaenia; most species appear to be oviparous, though some ovo-viviparous types are known. There are 24 genera and about 100 species, found in the warmer areas of Africa, Europe, Saudi Arabia, and North and South America, where they burrow in the soil, or inhabit termite or ant nests, feeding on small invertebrates. Little documentation on the captive care of these creatures is available which, due to their habits, do not constitute the idea of an ideal pet. However, the fact that so little is known about the life history of these interesting creatures, should inspire the serious herpetologist to further study.

Biology of the Snakes

The most outstanding and well known feature of the snakes is the fact that they are without limbs, although in some of the more primitive families a vestigeal pelvic girdle is present. In the Pythonidae, this manifests itself in the form of a pair of pre-anal 'claws' — larger in the male than the female — which seem to be of some significance in courtship. In spite of the presence of the pelvic girdle, there is no evidence to suggest close relationship with any lizard family, or even to the amphisbaenians, although it is almost certain that snakes arose from lizard ancestry.

The snake's body is typically elongated and the tail is of variable length. The surface is covered by overlapping scales which may be glossy or matt in appearance. A transparent spectacle over the eyes, known as the brill, is formed by fusion of the eyelids and the eye moves beneath this protective cover. There are no external ear openings but the presence of the auditory stapes indicates that the snake is stimulated by vibration through solid surfaces. This explains the sudden flight of wild snakes which have 'heard' the sound of approaching footsteps. The rami of the lower jaw are joined by elastic tissue which enables the snake to spread the mandible around large prey. For a similar reason the palatal bones are movably attached to the skull, which completely encloses the brain.

The typically forked tongue is retractile within a sheath and is a major sense organ used in connection with the organs of Jacobson, which are more highly developed in the snakes than in the lizards.

1 Tokay gecko, *Gekko gecko*, one of the largest species in the family Gekkonidae

2 Plumed basilisk, *Basiliscus plumifrons*. A bizzare lizard — ideal for the tropical rain forest terrarium

3 Green iguana, *Iguana iguana*, in a tastefully decorated display at London Zoo

4 Granite spiny lizard, *Sceloporus orcutti*; a desert species requiring high daytime temperatures

These paired organs are domed cavities lined with sensory epithelium and situated in the palate just below the nose. They are used to detect scent particles introduced into them by the tips of the very mobile forked tongue and function in much the same way as the nose. Interestingly, the normal sense of smell in most species is also fairly well developed.

The teeth are sharp and recurved, primarily adapted to seizing and holding the prey, rather than crushing and grinding as exhibited by lizards. They are present on the edges of the upper and lower jaw as well as on the palatal bones. The 100 or more teeth of the average snake are replaced in perpetual succession and those on the jaw are invariably pleurodont. In some of the more advanced snakes, certain teeth are adapted as venom fangs. Some colubrids have 2 or more fangs at the rear of the maxilla, enlarged and grooved to conduct poison from the venom glands situated in the cheek region (opistoglyphous) though most members of the family are non-venomous (aglyphous). The majority of rear fanged snakes are relatively harmless to man due to the weakness of the venom and the difficulty in engaging the venom fangs. However, two notable exceptions are the

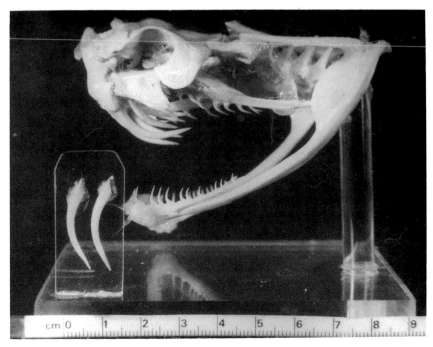

Prepared skull of a gaboon viper, *Bitis gabonica*. The large venom fangs and their replacements to the rear are clearly discernible. During post-mortem examination the two mounted fangs seen to the left were found in the duodenum, an indication that shed fangs are often swallowed, probably during feeding (*E. Elkan*)

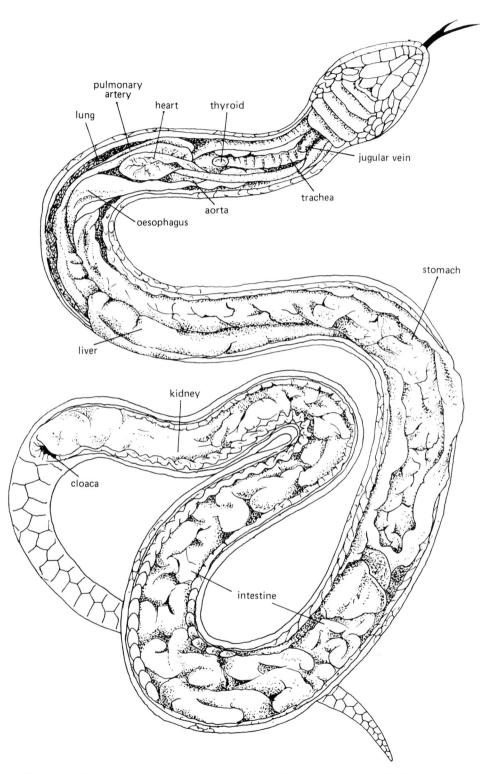

The internal anatomy of a typical female snake, with the major organs indicated

boomslang, *Dispholidus typus*, and the twig snake, *Thelotornis kirtlandi*, both of which have been known to cause death to humans by envenomation.

In the Elapidae and the Hydrophidae the paired venom fangs are fixed at the front of the maxilla (proteroglyphous) and are almost tubular, although the edges of the deep grooves are still visible. The venom is conducted through the canal and out of an aperture near to the point of the fang. In some species such as the ringhals, *Haemachatus haemachatus*, the aperture is directed forward and, by contraction of the venom gland, the snake is capable of directing jets of venom at the eyes of an aggressor, causing severe pain and temporary blindness.

The most efficient venom apparatus in snakes is that possessed by the family Viperidae. The hypodermic-like fangs have become completely canalised; they are the only teeth present on the maxilla and, unlike the fixed fangs of the proteroglyphs, they lie along the roof of the mouth during normal activity but can be rapidly brought forward by the rotation of the maxilla. The fangs of viperid snakes are usually relatively long, those of a large Gaboon viper being up to 3 cm (1in). Further notes on venomous snakes are given in chapter 7.

The flowing locomotion of most snakes is made possible by the accessory articulating facets of the vertebrae which allow the reptile to bend in any direction. Locomotion is achieved by lateral undulations of the dorsal muscles, coupled with rectilinear crawling, using the broad belly scales which are attached to the ribs by special

Types of fang structure in various groups of snakes

Aglyphous: non-venomous snakes; no poison groove or channel

Opistoglyphous: rear-fanged, colubrine snakes, with poison groove

Proteroglyphous: front-fanged elapid snakes, with poison channel

Solenoglyphous: front-fanged viperid snakes, with poison channel muscles. Some desert dwelling species such as the sidewinder, *Crotalus cerastes*, have developed a system of locomotion to enable them to move rapidly over loose sand. Such a system, known as sidewinding, involves 'walking' with coils of the body thrown over in loops.

Snakes have not perhaps achieved the variety of form exhibited by the lizards but have colonised most kinds of habitat. The most variable group is the Colubridae which includes terrestrial, arboreal and semi-aquatic forms. The Hydrophidae have colonised the sea, whilst numerous species in the more primitive families are primarily burrowers. Size ranges from 15cm (6in) in some of the burrowing snakes to 10m (33ft) in the pythons.

All snakes are carnivorous and include specialist and general feeders; some of the smaller varieties feed exclusively on invertebrates. There are those which are predominantly fish, frog, or bird eaters; others include egg eaters, *Dasypeltis scabra*; snail eaters, *Duberria lutrix*; centipede eaters; *Apparallactus capensis*; and even snake eaters, *Ophiophagus hannah* (the king cobra). Many snakes are capable of overpowering and swallowing prey of remarkable size through envenomation or constriction. Certain species, such as the pit vipers (Crotalinae) and some boids, are capable of detecting warm blooded prey by the use of heat sensitive pits, situated between the eye and nostril of the former, or around the lips of the latter. Experiments with such snakes have demonstrated that they are capable of detecting temperature differences of 0.2°C. It is believed that these snakes are able to form an image from such heat pits which enables them to identify prey even when, in experiment, they are 'blind-folded'.

Longevity

It is difficult to make any hard and fast statement about the longevity of lizards and snakes, but in general it can be said that the larger the species, the longer it will live. Certain species will live longer in captivity than in the wild; others, such as chamaeleons, for a considerably shorter time, although in the latter case this may reflect inadequate husbandry. Small lizards will live for 5 or 6 years, those of medium size up to 15 years, and larger lizards for 20 or more. Most snakes will live in excess of 10 years and some of the larger boids have been known to live for 30 or more.

3·ACCOMMODATION

A container in which living reptiles are kept is normally referred to as a vivarium or a terrarium. The author prefers the latter term as it distinguishes the difference between a container for terrestrial creatures, as opposed to those kept in an aquarium. Terrarium technology has advanced a long way since the advent of the glass fronted box, heated with a light bulb, and it is now possible to purchase ready made terraria with all systems electronically controlled.

However, most enthusiasts prefer to make their own, the advantages being: they can be made to a pattern suitable for the animals to be kept, to fit into a certain part of the home; and, not least, can save a lot of expense. Terraria can be manufactured from a host of different materials and, with a little artistic perception, can be made into an extremely attractive part of the decoration of the modern home. Choice of materials will reflect the type of reptiles to be kept; wood, for instance, would not be suitable for creatures requiring a humid environment, but is ideal for desert dwelling species.

Terraria can be loosely divided into a number of types, though there are no hard and fast rules and a certain amount of experimentation may have to be carried out with some species. The basic types may be divided into three as follows:

1 *The tall terrarium* This is greater in height than either the length or the breadth. Suitable for tree snakes, tree lizards, geckos, and other small arboreal reptiles.
2 *The low terrarium* This is greater in length than either the height or breadth. Suitable for terrestrial species such as many colubrid snakes, some boids, ground lizards, and those reptiles with limited climbing instincts.
3 *The aqua-terrarium* This may fall into categories 1 or 2, but incorporates a large area of water. Suitable for semi-aquatic reptiles such as some boids, monitor lizards, water dragons and water snakes.

In addition, terrarium types can be divided into further categories relating to the biological requirements of the species in question.

1 *The unheated dry terrarium* For species which normally live in the local climate or one similar, in heathland, or other such dry places.

In Europe, for instance, these could be *Lacerta vivipara*, *Podarcis muralis*, or *Vipera berus*.

2 *The unheated humid terrarium* For marsh and woodland species. In North America examples would be *Thamnophis sirtalis* and *Nerodia* species.

3 *The heated dry terrarium* For desert and semi-desert species a large number of reptiles would require this kind of accommodation.

4 *The heated humid terrarium* For tropical rain forest species of which there is an immense choice.

There are, of course, many borderline types, and the only way to decide what kind of accommodation is suitable for certain species is to obtain information on the habitat from a climatic atlas, or from other herpetologists successful with the species in question.

Wooden Terraria

Having decided on the type of reptiles to be kept, a terrarium can be purchased or made. Wooden terraria are useful for those species not requiring a great amount of humidity, and it is quite easy for the handyman to make a presentable display — which is basically a wooden box with a glass viewing panel at the front. It may be constructed from 5mm ($\frac{1}{4}$in) plywood glued and tacked to a 2×2cm ($\frac{3}{4}$in) batten framework, or, preferably, from 10mm ($\frac{1}{2}$in) plywood glued and tacked directly together without a frame. Chipboard and hardboard may also be used, but these materials will require a coat of primer, followed by an undercoat and two coats of good quality, lead-free, gloss paint to protect them from moisture. Plywood should be given a couple of coats of exterior (yacht) varnish. Whether or not the wood is stained before varnishing is left to individual taste.

The glass viewing panel, which will also double as the access door, may be mounted in a hinged frame, or slid into grooves — either vertically or horizontally. Adequate ventilation holes are drilled about one third of the way up the sides of the case and also in the roof. Alternatively, a large square, or rectangular, hole may be cut out at either end and covered with perforated zinc, or a wire gauze. Where small lizards or snakes are being kept pvc gauze will be adequate. The edges of the gauze can be secured and tidied up with a framework of half-round beading. Provision should be made for heating and lighting apparatus, which will be discussed later. Sometimes, it is possible to build the cage to fit round a plastic tray of the type used for cat litter or something similar. Such a tray would become a removable floor which would be hygienic, would hold the substrate, and would prevent moisture from damaging the wooden floor of the cage.

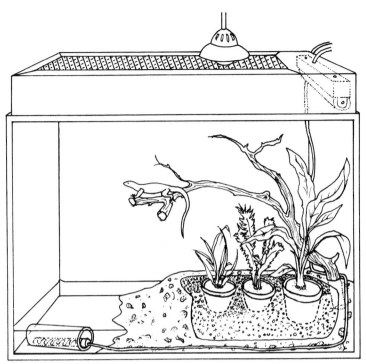

Large, glass terrarium set up for rain forest species. The plants are potted and sunk under gravel in special cavities in the concrete substrate. Additional water heating is supplied by an aquarium heater inside a plastic pipe, to avoid damage by the inmates

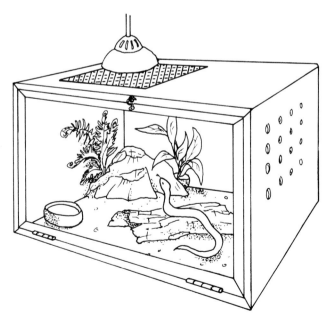

Easily constructed plywood terrarium. Note the extra ventilation holes in the upper part of the walls. Dangerous species require a secure lock on the lid

Glass Terraria

The availability of silicon rubber sealing compounds, which rev-
olutionised the construction of aquaria, is of tremendous value to the
terrarium keeper. Sheets of glass can be cemented together to form
a strong container of almost any desired shape. Moreover, sections
of the glass can be left out at the sides, or the back, so that ventilated
access doors of drilled plywood, plexiglass, or framed gauze can be
fitted.

As an example, a tall type terrarium $40\times40\times70$cm ($15\frac{3}{4}\times$
$15\frac{3}{4}\times27$in) high, to house a number of small geckos, tree
lizards, or tree snakes can be constructed from 5mm ($\frac{1}{4}$in) thick
strengthened glass. It is best to get a glass merchant to cut the sheets
to size, unless one is an adept glasscutter. Preferably, those edges
which will be left exposed after construction should be ground smooth
to eradicate the risk of cut fingers. The following sheets will be
required:

1 base	40×40cm	($15\frac{3}{4}\times15\frac{3}{4}$in)	
2 sides	40×70cm	($15\frac{3}{4}\times27$in)	
1 front	40×70.5cm	($15\frac{3}{4}\times27\frac{1}{4}$)	To allow for thickness
1 rear pane	40×15.5cm	($15\frac{3}{4}\times6\frac{1}{8}$in)	of the base
1 rear pane	40×15cm	($15\frac{3}{4}\times5\frac{7}{8}$in)	

In addition, a sheet of 5mm ($\frac{1}{4}$in) plywood is required for the
access/ventilation door at the back. Plexiglass or clear acrylic can
also be used for the door, which can be slid into position on plastic
runners cemented in position on the top and the bottom of the open
part (see figure). Whether of plywood or synthetic materials, the door
should be drilled in a symmetric pattern with a series of small holes
to act as ventilators.

Taking a firm, flat surface, preferably covered with an old blanket,
or several sheets of newspaper, lay the base sheet down. Apply a
continuous strip of aquarium sealer (tubes of this sealer with a special
applicator nozzle may be obtained from aquarist's suppliers) along
the bottom edge of one of the side panes and place this in position
on top of one of the base edges. Some assistance will be required to
hold this in position while a further strip of sealer is layered along
the outer front edges of the side and base panes, ready to receive the
front which is held in position with adhesive tape. Next, cement the
other side panel into position and again hold it in place with adhesive
tape. Finally, fix the lower and upper back panels into place, and
ensure that all the parts are firmly taped together, before leaving it
to stand for a couple of hours to allow the sealer to partially set. For
added strength, a continuous, triangular section strip of sealer should
be applied along all internal joints. The sealer can be smoothed over

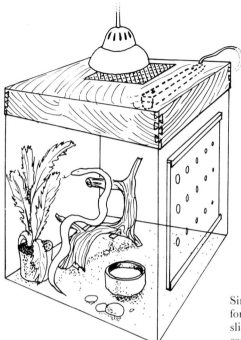

Simple, all-glass terrarium suitable for many species. Note the ventilated, sliding acrylic door and the fluorescent tube set in the wooden lid.

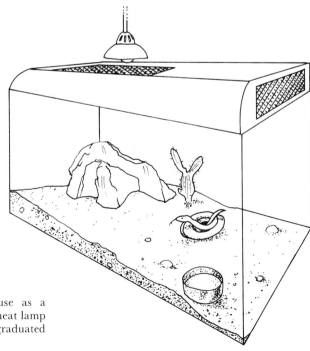

Aquarium converted for use as a desert type terrarium. The heat lamp is set at one end to create a graduated temperature scale

The common curly-tailed iguana, *Leiocephalus carinatus* is suitable for the small terrarium

with a wet finger, and any sealer which gets onto the viewing panels should be allowed to set, when it may easily be removed with a razor blade.

When using sealing compounds, ensure that you are working in an adequately ventilated area as the acetic acid vapours can be unpleasant and overpowering. The sealer should be perfectly set after twenty-four hours, when the adhesive tape may be removed, the excess sealer scraped away, and the glass thoroughly cleaned and polished from both sides.

The lid for the terrarium should be made to fit over the top of the main container and lips, just below the edges of the lid will prevent it from sliding too far down. The depth of the lid will depend on the size and type of heating/lighting apparatus required but 15cm (6in) should be adequate. The lid can be made of 5mm ($\frac{1}{4}$in) plywood and constructed so that the inner edges are a fraction over 40×41cm ($15\frac{3}{4}\times16$in) to give a good fit. Holes are drilled in the top for ventilation purposes. The lid can be painted, or varnished to make it look more attractive, and strips of plastic, or vinyl, of a similar colour may be attached around the bottom of the container to conceal the substrate.

Acrylic sheeting may also be used for terrarium construction but the drawback with this material is that it scratches easily and will not stand up to regular cleaning without an opaque film of fine scratches forming on the surfaces.

Built-in Terraria

One of the most satisfying types of home terrarium is that which is made from substantial materials, such as bricks, concrete blocks, or timber. It may be built in an alcove, or be free standing in the living area, or in a conservatory, greenhouse, or spare room. The advantages of such terraria, which are especially recommended for the larger species, such as boids, varanids, or large iguanids, are that they can be constructed to match the internal decoration. With a solid concrete base, the pond can thus be constructed in the floor; rockwork can be built up to form artificial cliff faces, incorporating controllable hiding places, and plant troughs can be built both in and at strategic points outside the terrarium. There is no limit to the designs which can be used and some of the best terraria seen by the author have been designed and built by the owners. Such designs have included a tropical rain forest exhibit — complete with a waterfall, lush plants, and underwater viewing. Fish may be kept in the specially filtered and treated pondwater, whilst tree lizards and frogs populate the land area.

As an example of a built-in terrarium for Indian pythons, the following method may be used. Sizes given can of course be varied, depending on available space and the type of reptiles to be kept. An alcove between the fireplace and the wall can be used. Such an alcove 2m (6½ft) long by 1.5m (5ft) wide would have three walls built, one abutting the fireplace wall, one at the opposite end abutting the other wall, and one in the centre. The walls can be about 80cm (31½in) high, depending on the required height of the cage floor. A piece of 10mm (½in) thick plywood is rested on the walls to cover the whole area, with the exception of a strip about 2–3cm (¾–1in) wide at each end to allow the floor concrete to come into contact with the brick wall. For similar purposes, large holes may be drilled in the plywood along the line of the centre wall. A piece of shuttering ply about 8cm (3in) wide is attached to the floor board all the way along its length to provide support for the concrete floor when it is poured. This can be screwed on to lugs attached to the floor board and can then be easily removed after the concrete has set. At the point where the deepest part of the pool is to be, a hole should be drilled to take the pond drainpipe, which should be a minimum of 2.5cm (1in) in diameter. Arrangement should be made for the drain hole to take a sink or bath waste with a standard plug. Alternatively, a gate valve can be fitted to the pipe beneath the floor. It will be necessary to take the drain out through the wall of the house to an existing runaway. The drain hole should be firmly plugged with a rolled up sheet of newspaper during the construction, to prevent concrete fouling it up.

To keep the area waterproof, and to prevent the floor board from rotting, a sheet of heavy grade polythene of the type used by builders for damp proofing, is placed over the whole area and up the walls for a distance of about 10cm (4in). A small hole will need to be cut for the drain pipe. A concrete mix of one part cement, two parts sharp sand, and four parts pea size gravel — mixed with water to form a pliable consistency — is then poured to form a floor about 5cm (2 in) thick. For added strength, a panel of steel mesh can be placed in the centre of the concrete, taking care that it does not come through the surface. The concrete can be tamped down level by using a piece of flat wood, but need not be smoothed over as the second layer will cover it.

Allow forty-eight hours for the first layer to set before proceeding further. The pond should be constructed from fairly dry concrete, and the surrounding floor should slope down to it, to facilitate cleaning. If gravel is to be used as a substrate, a lip should be constructed around the pond, through which a small pipe passes at the lowest point of the floor. This will facilitate drainage when washing down. Ensure that the drain hole is at the lowest part of the pond, and ensure that the drain joint is waterproof by using a sealing compound. Parts of the floor and the walls can have natural rocks built into them. Alternatively, artificial rocks can be made by sculpturing concrete with a trowel and smoothing it into shape with a paint brush. Such techniques require a little practice but are soon learnt; some splendid natural looking rock formations have been made using old housebricks and mortar. A final cement wash can be applied over the whole area. Such a wash can be made from one part cement, one part fine sand, and a little colouring agent. The wash should be mixed to the consistency of thick pea soup, adding more water, or cement, and stirring constantly until the desired density is reached. It can be applied with a large paintbrush, which must be washed out in clean water each time it becomes clogged. Excess water should be squeezed out of the brush before proceeding. By using small quantities of other cement colours as one goes along, a very natural looking surface can be created.

The front of the cage can be constructed with a timber framework, into which framed glass doors are fitted, either to open on hinges, or to be fitted into runners. Facilities for ventilation should be incorporated in the bottom and the top of the cage to allow convection currents. A convenient method of heating is to have a radiator under the terrarium and a mesh covered space between the front edge of the floor and the framework. The doors concealing the space below the cage should have ventilation holes so that the heated air rising into the interior is replaced. The lighting and possible radiant heating apparatus can be set into the roof part of the cage behind strong mesh.

With the enormous variety of terrarium types, it is impossible to give more than a few basic ideas here. The figures will provide more detailed information on the construction of various home terraria but it is advisable to go and examine fellow enthusiasts' cages and discuss the pros and cons before embarking on a construction project.

Terrarium Heating

With most species of lizards and snakes, whether from dry or humid climates, supplementary heating of one form or another will be required. There are as many different kinds of heating apparatus as there are terraria and the types will also vary, depending on the size of the cages. For a number of small cages housing snakes, geckos, or other reptiles not requiring high light or radiant heat intensity, it is sufficient to store the cages in a room which is heated to the required temperature. Such a system is ideal for breeding rooms where large numbers of small species, or juveniles, are kept in converted lunch boxes, or other plastic cages into which adequate ventilation holes have been drilled.

In more substantial terraria, heating apparatus will be necessary. Such apparatus should be installed and tested before the decoration is completed and the animals added. It is best to have a thermometer inside the cage and to leave the heating apparatus on for at least four hours to ensure that the temperature range is correct, or whether adjustments will have to be made. Remember that some species adjust their temperature by thermoregulation so that a range of temperatures should be provided. This can be achieved by having the heat source at one end of the terrarium only, so that various levels of heat are available from one end of the terrarium to the other. Most species require a reduction in temperature at night, and in the majority of cases it is a simple matter just to switch off the apparatus; the room temperature of the average household is adequate. However, where cages are kept in unheated outhouses subdued night-time heating will be necessary.

The use of thermostats and time switches can be very useful and will ensure a regularity of night/day temperatures which are not so

The crevice spiny lizard, *Sceloporus pointsettia*

Sizzle Stone

- Decorative heating device provides your reptiles with year-round warmth
- Available in three sizes

a

Hot Block

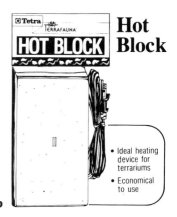

- Ideal heating device for terrariums
- Economical to use

b

A Sizzle Stones® are a decorative rock produced around low voltage heating elements.
B Hot Blocks® are a heating device functioning by placing gravel over it.

easy to achieve manually. Seasonal adjustments will still, however, be necessary.

Ordinary tungsten light bulbs have long been used to heat terraria. They have certain advantages in that they are cheap, supply light as well as heat, and come in various sizes. The required temperatures can be acquired by experimenting with numbers of bulbs of various wattages. A useful method of night-time heating is a bulb of low wattage — coloured blue or red to minimise the light. The main disadvantage of light bulbs is that the quality of light emitted is unsuitable both for the terrarium plants and many species of reptiles, although it is quite adequate for use as supplementary lighting.

Infra-red lamps of the type used in poultry hatcheries, or by pig-breeders, are very useful for large terraria. Such lamps have built in reflectors which direct the heat into a limited area and are useful for heating up basking sites. White lamps with a similar function are also available. Special lamps produced for the indoor propagation of plants are ideal for heating certain areas of the cage as well as providing light. The temperature of the glass bulbs of some of these lamps becomes extremely high and care should be taken not to splash them with water or they will shatter. It is also preferable to install such lamps outside the terrarium, behind a wire mesh, to prevent the animals being burnt by touching them. Some snakes seem to be remarkably stupid when it comes to heat sources and have been known to receive severe burns after coiling themselves around the lamps. The temperature of the surfaces below the lamps can be raised or lowered by moving the lamp up or down. When using any form of radiant lamp, care should be taken not to direct the beam on to plants, or the foliage will desiccate and die off.

Another kind of heater which is very popular in the United States is the Sizzle Stone®, the only patented terrarium heater. Its natural rock-like appearance makes it an ideal terrarium accessory. It comes in several sizes to meet the requirements of almost every size terrarium and its creatures.

A simple but effective heater and humidifier (known in Germany as the Tofohr-Ofen [oven] after the person who invented it), consists of a simple light bulb mounted inside a tin-can. Lugs are cut in the top of the can and bent outwards so that it can be screwed, open top downwards, over a hole cut in the terrarium base. The light bulb fitting is fixed to a removable bracket under the cage so that the bulb passes partially into the can. A piece of clay drainpipe, or a large clay flower pot, is placed over the can and, in the case of the former, a wire mesh lid is placed over the top. A small dish of water placed on top of the can will prevent 'dust burning' and provide humidity. The water should be topped up at regular intervals, using a 'squeezer'.

The Hot Block® is a useful terrarium heating device which is placed under a gravel substrata and dissipates heat throughout the surface area. Hot Blocks come in a variety of sizes and heating capabilities, depending on the size of the terrarium and the demands of the creatures. Another idea is to have an aquarium heater contained in a jar of water in the terrarium, the cable passing through a hole in the ventilated lid; such an apparatus will provide humidity as well as heat. All substrate heaters should be arranged to provide local heating in certain areas so that the inmates can select their own preferred temperatures. Another idea is to have an aquarium heater contained in a jar of water in the terrarium, the cable passing through a hole in the ventilated lid; such an apparatus will provide humidity as well as heat. All substrate heaters should be arranged to provide local heating in certain areas so that the inmates can select their own preferred temperatures.

Lighting

Adequate lighting is just as important to captive lizards and snakes as correct heating. Light cycles are necessary for all species, whether nocturnal or diurnal, and some require natural sunlight, or a good substitute. When one considers that the intensity of light provided by a 40 watt tungsten bulb at a distance of one metre (approx. three and a quarter feet) is only about one three-thousandth of that provided by the full summer sun, it can be seen that some difficulty will arise in finding a good substitute. Even the so called 'daylight' tubes provide only about one five-hundredth of natural sunlight intensity, while a high wattage mercury-vapour lamp will emit roughly one hundred and fiftieth. It is, therefore, an impossibility to artificially

Giant zonure, *Cordylus giganteus*. Also known as the sungazer, or girdled lizard, this species settles and breeds well in captivity

reproduce natural sunlight intensity. However, natural light should not be ignored when choosing a site for your terrarium. It may be placed near a window which receives direct sunlight for not more than four hours per day; any more than this will bring a danger of overheating. Morning or late afternoon sunlight is preferable for the confined area of the terrarium, so an ideal situation would be near a west or east facing window.

As a result of experimentation in recent years, much progress has been made in the field of artificial lighting for terraria. When it was realised that the most important part of sunlight to reptiles was the infra-red and ultra-violet rays, the former for heat absorption, the latter to aid in the production of vitamin D_3, some herpetologists had the bright idea of using a combination of infra-red lamps and broad spectrum fluorescent tubes, which had originally been manufactured for horticultural use. Infra-red lamps have already been discussed in the section on heating and it is only the white-type lamps which emit any appreciable light, although all infra-red lamps are suitable for use with basking animals.

Ultra-violet lamps are of limited use in the terrarium, although some herpetologists recommend that certain species of basking lizards and snakes be exposed to ultra-violet rays for a few minutes each week. Exposure should never be for more than twenty minutes at a time and not more than twice per week; prolonged exposure can cause incurable damage to the animal's skin. In small doses, however,

5 Bearded dragon, *Amphibolurus barbatus*; a popular Australian agamid

6 Water dragon, *Physignathus cocincinus*. This colourful agamid comes from south-east Asia

7 and 8 Jackson's chamaeleon, *Chamaeleo jacksoni*. The female (above) lacks the three facial 'horns' seen in the male (below) and displays the colour variation

ultra-violet rays have proven to enhance the colour and general health of many species.

Broad spectrum fluorescent tubes are much safer to use than ultra-violet lamps. They emit small quantities of ultra-violet rays of an intensity unlikely to cause any damage to the reptiles as well as a reasonable quota of white light. The use of such fluorescent tubes in recent years has considerably improved the captive husbandry of many species which were hitherto classed as difficult. There are several makes of these tubes which come under such trade names as 'Gro-lux', 'Day-glo', or 'Tru-lite', and most large lighting companies produce one form or another. Manufacturers are usually pleased to provide specification details of lamps available and it is both useful and interesting to obtain information leaflets. Broad spectrum tubes are indispensible if plants are to be grown within the terrarium, which is why earlier keepers, with their tungsten bulb lighting, normally dispensed with plants altogether after a few abortive attempts to keep them alive.

Other forms of lighting which may be considered in large terraria are mercury-vapour and halogen lamps, both of which emit a greater intensity of light than any other artificial light forms. Such lamps may have a wattage of 500 or more and emit a high quota of radiant heat, so are unsuitable for small terraria unless suspended well above the outside of the cage. The use of such lamps will promote lush plant growth as long as the distance is great enough to prevent desiccation of the foliage.

When setting up a terrarium with heating and lighting apparatus, it is well to consider the safety aspects. Electricity and water, together, constitute a real danger and care should be taken to see that all parts of the electrical appliances are properly insulated and waterproof. If in doubt about the wiring, obtain the advice or services of a professional electrician. It is better to be safe than sorry.

Humidity

Humidity, or the lack of it, is just as important in the terrarium as heating and lighting. For obvious reasons, creatures native to arid environments will not survive for long in a tropical rain forest terrarium; conversely, it would be foolish to expect a creature from a damp woodland to survive in a desert terrarium. With regard to humidity, it is probably easier to keep desert creatures than those from damp environments as the forms of heating and lighting in the average terrarium will automatically create a dry habitat, provided only a small drinking water vessel is used.

For creatures requiring a humid environment it is necessary to provide some means of artificial humidification. This is not so dif-

ficult as it may sound. In an aqua-terrarium, where there is a large
water surface area, natural evaporation of the water will create its
own humidity levels, which will be enhanced by the action of the
animals entering and leaving the water. The addition of an aquarium
heater to the water vessel will create further slow evaporation; this
can be increased by using an aquarium aerator, consisting of an air
diffuser stone in the water supplied with air through a narrow gauge
plastic pipe from an air pump. Small air pumps can be bought
inexpensively and can be used for ventilation purposes, as well as
for the creation of extra humidity. Another method of increasing
humidity levels is to use the Tofohr-oven. With large built-in terraria
a waterfall running over rocks, and controlled by a small circulatory
pump, will automatically raise the humidity in the cage. The simplest
method is just to spray the interior of the cage and the plant foliage
with water at regular intervals, preferably, at least twice per day.
The plants themselves will benefit from such spraying, as will the
animals — some of which will make water droplets their sole drinking
source.

Whatever method of humidification is used, it must be remembered
that reptiles still require a dry area where they can bask. A permanently wet environment will lead to skin disorders in many species,
so ensure that there are sufficient dry surfaces for the animals to seek
out should they so wish. Another point to bear in mind is that in
many habitats the humidity varies from season to season. In some
tropical climates a season of heavy rain is followed by a relatively
dry one, and it is wise to endeavour to reproduce a similar effect in
the terrarium where appropriate. Such seasonal humidity changes
may have a bearing on the reproductive cycles of some species.

Ventilation

Along with heating, lighting, and humidity, ventilation is another
important factor in the terrarium. Inadequate ventilation leads to
build up of carbon dioxide in the terrarium base; permanent dampness and its associated problems; and an increase in possibly harmful
micro-organisms. In basic terrarium construction, provision must
always be made for adequate ventilation, whether by holes drilled
through the walls at differing heights, or by mesh covered panels. It
is always advisable to have a ventilating area near the base of the
terrarium, as well as near the top, to allow regular exchange of the
total air content of the cage. Additional apparatus for creating air
movement will not normally be necessary as the convection currents
created by the rising air from the heated areas will be adequate for
regular air replacement. An aquarium aerator will supply extra
ventilation for a small terrarium and the air pipe need not necessarily

be in the water if a lower humidity is required. For terraria kept in stuffy living rooms, particularly where the owners are smokers, it will pay to have the fresh air drawn from outside. This can be passed over an underfloor heater before it enters the terrarium through a special ventilator.

Fresh air is free and beneficial to animals and plants, so every opportunity should be taken to use it. On warm days, portable terraria may be placed outside, by open windows, or on balconies, but ensuring that the sun does not shine directly through glass. The type of green shading used for greenhouse roofs can be used over the terrarium glass. Dappled sunlight entering through the mesh of the terrarium lid will do no harm, in fact it will be extremely beneficial to some species of lizards and snakes.

Greenhouse Accommodation

Many herpetologists like to keep free-range reptiles in a heated greenhouse, conservatory, or a small purpose-built tropical house. The advantages of this are manyfold and far outweigh the dis-advantages — the main one being the expense of creating the right environment in a large area. However, once this is achieved, such an environment is particularly suitable for tropical rain forest species. A miniature jungle can be grown and high levels of humidity can be maintained by the use of a waterfall and regular damping-down. Basking areas can be placed in several strategic positions using heat lamps. The background temperature should not drop below 15°C, and the reptiles will be able to find their own higher levels by basking.

Windows and ventilation holes must be covered with a suitably sized mesh to prevent escapes. Pipes and other heating appliances should be caged-in to prevent the animals burning themselves and from disappearing into the various cavities associated with such systems. All hiding places should be accessible and controllable, as it will be necessary to catch up some of the inhabitants from time to time. With adequate space, it will be possible to keep a number of groups of compatible species. A group of agamid or iguanid tree lizards, for example, will be able to behave in an almost natural manner and each male will be able to seek out his own territory. The proud owner of such a set-up will be able to spend many hours seated in his very own jungle, studying the interesting habits of his charges. Breeding should easily be achieved in such an environment, although the eggs will probably have to be removed for artificial incubation. If enough small lizards are bred it may be possible to keep a pair of small, lizard-eating tree snakes in the same enclosure, if you can bear the thought of some of your lizards being eaten.

Outdoor Enclosures

Probably the most satisfactory method of keeping lizards and snakes is in an outdoor reptiliary. Species native to the area in which the reptiliary is built will have no climatic problems whatsoever and it is possible to keep many subtropical species outdoors all the year round, in temperate climates, provided satisfactory hibernacula are provided. Such animals will breed quite easily in the summer months, but it will be necessary to gather up the eggs for artificial incubation. Even tropical species will benefit from a holiday in an outdoor reptiliary during the hotter part of the summer, and the exposure to natural sunlight will be of great value to their health.

A basic reptiliary consists of a walled enclosure with a firmly packed foundation to a ground depth of at least 50cm (19½in) to prevent the inmates from burrowing out. Size will depend on the amount of space available, and on the number and species of lizards, or snakes, to be kept. For most smaller species the wall height need be no greater than 90cm (36in), but of course snakes in excess of this length are not likely to stay around for very long! The top of the wall should have an overhang at least 15cm (6in) wide to prevent escapes over the top; alternatively, a continuous row of glossy ceramic tiles around the top of the inside wall will prevent escapes.

It is usually best to leave a moat about 60cm (24in) wide around the inside of the wall, and to keep this free of debris. The body of earth removed from the foundations is piled up in the centre of the enclosure to form a mound, with adequate south facing slopes (in the Southern Hemisphere, of course, the opposite will apply). During construction, ponds, waterfalls, rocks, and cliff faces can be incorporated as well as, if necessary, hibernacula. These may consist of plastic food containers with a hole cut in the side, into which is introduced a length of plastic pipe of a gauge sufficient in size for the reptiles to gain access. The waterproof containers are loosely packed with dry, sphagnum moss, hay, or wood shavings and then buried about 50cm (19½in) deep into the mound. The entrance tunnel should slope slightly downwards from the container to prevent water from entering and flooding the chamber. The end of the pipe can be concealed with a number of rocks cemented together, just leaving a fissure through which the reptiles will pass.

The reptiliary can be decorated with plenty of rocks, flat stones under which the more retiring creatures can bask, and one or two rotting logs which will provide more hiding places and a supply of insect food. The area can be planted with a number of attractive alpine and rock plants, mostly of the low, ground hugging variety, but a few thickly foliaged low shrubs will provide climbing areas for some species. Plenty of flowering plants will attract a range of insects to the reptiliary and it will be interesting to see the inmates hunting them. It may still be necessary to provide additional food and a daily ration of mealworms, crickets, or similar will soon become expected by lizards, which will wait at the feeding point.

A number of sunny, plant free sandy areas should be provided for some species to lay eggs. For many snakes and some lizards a small mound of grass clippings can be provided. Eggs will often be laid in such a medium which produces its own heat source through decay. Close watch should be kept for mating and egglaying activities in order that the eggs can be collected as soon as possible for artificial incubation. Maintenance of such a reptiliary is minimal and consists mainly of pruning the plants back and ensuring there are no over-hanging branches, or growths up the inner walls which would provide escape routes for the inmates.

Terrarium Plants and Decoration

Having discussed the various types of terraria and enclosures suitable for lizards and snakes, a few notes on the type of decoration used in indoor terraria will not go amiss. Plants, rocks, tree branches, and substrate materials, other than a sheet of absorbent paper, are not strictly necessary. Many species have been successfully bred in a terrarium containing only a sheet of newspaper on the floor, a brick to aid in sloughing or to bask on, a dish of water, and a cornflake box in which to hide. Indeed, where large numbers of reptiles are kept for breeding, or experimental purposes, this is the most practical way of keeping them. However, the average herpetologist will want to have at least one decorative terrarium in his living area, in which he can create a facsimile of the reptiles' habitat.

Substrate Materials In the dry terrarium for small reptiles, coarse sand, or a mixture of sand and peat can be used as a floor covering. Fine sand, or silver sand, should never be used as this will stick to the animals' skin — particularly after they have crawled through the water container — and cake between the scales causing sloughing problems later. For larger reptiles, and for humid terraria, it is recommended that clean gravel is used. This should be thoroughly washed and dried out before use. Gravel and shingle is available in many grades and types ranging from 2–3mm ($\frac{1}{4}$in) aquarium shingle up to 10–15mm ($\frac{1}{2}$–$\frac{3}{4}$in) granite chips. It is interesting to look around and discover new types of substrate material for the terrarium; there are various kinds of crushed rock of many colours which can look very attractive. It is advisable to obtain enough so that a spare stock is available to use at cleaning time, which should be about once per month.

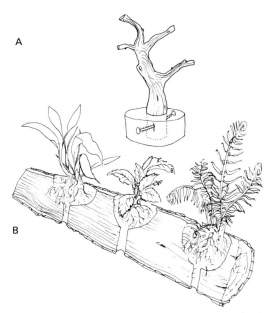

A method of stabilising a tree branch, by casting a concrete 'foot' around it. Nails in the base of the branch and totally embedded in the cement will add strength. B attractive epiphytic displays can be made by hollowing out cavities in logs for planting. Suitable for the humid terrarium, the diagram shows an example in longitudinal section

Tree Branches For most reptiles, even those which do not climb a great deal, a tree branch in the terrarium is both attractive to look at and will provide exercise for the inmates. Branches of bizarre shape are best and, in particular, driftwood from the sea shore is most attractive as it will have been bleached, weathered, and smoothed down by the action of sun, sea, and sand. All wood collected for the terrarium should be thoroughly scrubbed, washed, and dried before use. Hollow logs and branches are useful as hiding places for some species, but ensure that such hiding places are accessible to you. With a little carpentry, it is possible to fashion controllable places of seclusion. Corkwood bark is a useful item for many terraria and can form an attractive backing to the container; it may also be used to conceal potted plants. For small arboreal species, a sturdy tree branch is essential and will also provide a support for creeping plants.

Rocks These can be used to good effect in the terrarium as basking areas, hiding places, and as an aid to sloughing. Rocks of the type used in aquaria, and available in the stores, are often ideal. Alternatively, natural rocks can be collected on location. Whether these are jagged rocks or large weathered pebbles is a matter of taste, but they should be arranged in such a way that they cannot fall down and injure the reptiles. In large terraria, where a great number of rocks are used, it is best to cement these together, leaving only controllable hiding places, or great problems will ensue when the reptiles need to be removed.

The author and others have experimented with lightweight artificial rocks consisting of blocks of expanded polystyrene covered with a 10mm ($\frac{1}{2}$in) layer of cement. Such rocks have great advantages over conventional ones; they can be made to fit exactly into corners so that there are no hiding places left for elusive reptiles or parasites; controlled hiding places can be incorporated; and being extremely light, they are easy to move about and ideal for the smaller terrarium. Expanded polystyrene is an insulating or packing material, available in sheets of various thicknesses. Thicker chunks can be made by passing pieces of stiff wire through several layers of the material and bending them over at the end. The ·required shape is roughly fashioned by breaking or cutting off pieces, and then it is covered with a layer of about 10mm ($\frac{1}{2}$in) thick cement mortar, containing a plasticising agent. A suitable mix is one part cement, two parts fine sand, and plasticising agent to the manufacturer's instructions.

The materials are mixed slowly together with water until the required pliability is reached, and then it is plastered over the exposed surfaces of the polystyrene. The surface can be smoothed into shape with a damp paintbrush and, with skilful use of a trowel, various authentic looking rock formations can be sculpted. The part fitting into the corners need not be cemented over and the job can be done in situ, or an artificial 90° corner can be made from two pieces of plank. Free

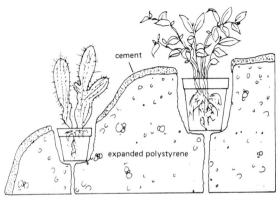

A cross section of artificial rockwork, made from expanded polystyrene, covered with cement. Cavities and drainage holes are left for potted plants

standing rocks should be covered on all sides except the bottom which will be resting on the terrarium floor. Some excellent controllable hiding places can be made by making two rocks, slightly hollowed out inside, and fitted exactly on top of each other, leaving a couple of access holes for the reptiles to crawl into. The joint between the two rocks can be sculpted to look like a stratum, or natural rock fault. A colouring agent can be added to the cement before construction or a cement wash, as described earlier, can be used. Allow at least forty-eight hours in a cool atmosphere for the cement to set before moving the rock.

Plants There is no doubt that plants in the terrarium add that subtle finishing touch to the decoration, particularly if it is to be the showpiece of the living room or wherever. However, plants are not easy to keep in good condition in the terrarium — sometimes even more difficult than the animals! Plants also have requirements of heat, light, humidity and ventilation depending on the species. In general, many kinds of exotic house plants are suitable and should be looked after as recommended by the supplier, or as described in a good book about exotic plants. It is best to keep all plants potted, and the pots can be concealed behind little piles of rocks. If you are using artificial rocks an advantage is that cavities can be fashioned which exactly take the pots. The normal potting soil should be covered with a fairly heavy shingle (but depending on the size of the reptiles) to prevent the animals digging the roots up. Another advantage of potted plants is that they can easily be removed at cleaning time, and if a spare plant of each type is kept they can be swapped over at regular intervals; whilst one is in the terrarium, the other is recuperating in the greenhouse, or on the windowsill. The following is a brief list of plants found to be reasonably hardy in the terrarium, provided the correct conditions are provided.

1 Plants For The Heated Dry Terrarium

Name	Origin	Remarks
Aeonium canariense	Canary Islands	Requires dry, stony soil.
A. domesticum	North Africa	as above
Agave americana	Mediterranean region	Requires a little more moisture than the previous species
A. schidigera	Mediterranean region	as above
Aloe arista	South Africa	as above
A. ferox	South Africa	as above
A. variegata	South Africa	as above
Chamaerops humilis	Mediterranean region	as above

Name	Origin	Remarks
Echinocactus species	North America	as above
Euphorbia milii	Madagascar	as above
Ferocactus species	North America	as above
Gasteria maculata	South Africa	as above
Haworthia fasciata	South Africa	as above
Hedera helix	Cosmopolitan	Regular watering
Kalanchoe blossfeldiana	East Africa	as above
Mammillaria species	North America	Semi-desert
Myrtus communis	Mediterranean region	Regular watering
Opuntia species	N and S America	Semi-desert
Sansevieria cylindrica	Central Africa	as above
S. trifasciata	Central Africa	as above
Sempervivum arachnoideum	Mediterranean region	as above

2 Plants For The Heated Humid Terrarium

Name	Origin	Remarks
Aechmea species	Central and S America	Epiphytic
Aglaonema boscheanus	S E Asia	Marsh plant
Alocasia cuprea	S E Asia	Marsh plant
Anthurium species	Central and S America	Rain forest
Anubias lanceolata	West Africa	Marsh plant
Aphelandra aurantiaca	Mexico	Forest
Begonia species	India	Forest
Billbergia species	S America	Rain forest
Calathea zebrina	S America	Rain forest
Cissus discolor	Java	Rain forest
Coffea liberica	Central Africa	Forest
Coleus pumilus	S E Asia	Forest
Codiaetum variegata	Indonesia	Rain forest
Dieffenbachia maculata	S America	Rain forest
Dracaena godseffiana	West Africa	Rain forest
Ficus species	S E Asia	Forest
Maranta species	S America	Rain forest
Monstera deliciosa	S America	Rain forest
Pandanus pygmaeus	Madagascar	Forest
Peperomia species	Cosmopolitan	Rain forest
Philodendron species	S America	Rain forest
Platycerium grande	S E Asia	Epiphytic
Saintpaulia ionantha	East Africa	Rain forest
Syngonium species	Central and S America	Rain forest
Tillandsia species	Central and S America	Epiphytic
Vriesia species	Tropical S America	Epiphytic

4·GENERAL CARE

The general care of any captive animal commences on the day it is acquired and continues daily on a routine basis. Anyone desiring to keep lizards or snakes in confinement has full responsibility for their welfare and must ensure that the time, patience, and ongoing interest are available before obtaining specimens. Reptiles are not time consuming in their maintenance, once the basic terrarium has been set up, and four or five hours per week should be adequate for routine cleaning jobs.

Selection and Acquisition of Specimens

Of the several thousand different species of lizards and snakes, relatively few are usually available at any one time; and this will depend on such things as season, the country in which one lives, and conservation status of the reptiles in question. Most countries have their specialist dealers in amphibians and reptiles and many aquarist's suppliers carry a few species. It will certainly pay to spend a few days shopping around before making a decision. Always avoid those premises which are untidy, dirty and have masses of smelly unhealthy looking specimens in small cages. Unfortunately, such premises still exist, but they are more than compensated for by professional dealers who really care for their stock, presenting it in clean attractive terraria and being able to answer specific questions about individual species.

Always examine the stock very carefully before purchasing, looking for signs of mite or ticks on the specimens, or in the cages. Choose those with a clean unbroken skin devoid of any unsloughed patches. Ensure that the reptile is alert, clear-eyed and plump. Ask if it is feeding regularly (although most dealers will affirm this whether it is or not), and examine the mouth and vent for any sign of inflammation which could indicate disease. If possible, have a trial handling session in the shop to make sure one is competent in restraining it.

Another, probably better, way of obtaining stock is to approach breeders of captive specimens. The best way to find out who is breeding what is to join a herpetological society and discuss one's requirements with fellow members. Quite often, breeders will advertise their surplus stock in the society newsletter, giving a telephone number or contact address. The big advantage of home bred stock is that it is more likely to settle in the new terrarium, is less likely to be diseased or infested with parasites, and one will have the knowledge that another animal has not been taken from the wild.

The third method of obtaining stock is one which must be considered with great caution. Collecting from the wild is not as readily possible as it used to be, and in many countries all species are protected; in others, only licensed collectors may capture specimens. Where only certain species are protected it may be possible to collect some of the others. Never collect more than desired for one's own requirements; it can be an offence in some countries to capture specimens for resale. In any case, such collecting is unethical and should be left to the licensed dealers. One advantage of collecting such specimens is that one will be able to see *exactly* the type of habitat and prepare the terrarium accordingly. Before attempting to collect from the wild, be aware of the national and local legislation appertaining to the area in question.

Transport

The transport and despatch of reptiles is a subject which requires a great deal of thought. All too often animals are lost in transit due to thoughtless packing. The most satisfactory method of transporting the majority of species is in individual cloth bags, packed in stout cardboard or wooden boxes. Should the packages have to travel through cold climates it is advisable to have them lined with an insulating material such as expanded polystyrene. Always select the quickest and most direct route and despatch by rail or road. The practice of sending small reptiles through the post should be avoided where possible.

When purchasing stock, it is advisable to collect it whenever this is convenient. Not only will one have a chance of examining the specimens first, but one will also be able to ensure that they reach their destination without mishap. Very small reptiles, such as geckos, small lizards, and snakes, may be packed directly into small rigid plastic or cardboard boxes, with a little shredded paper or dry sphagnum moss to cushion them should they get tossed about. All larger lizards and snakes are best packed individually in cloth bags, which should be tied at the neck and through which the reptiles will comfortably be able to breathe. Due to the low metabolic rate of reptiles, it is not necessary to provide them with food or water for the short journeys which they are liable to experience today. Each bag should have a label tied onto it giving the name of the contents, and the outer container should be clearly marked with the address of the consignee and the consignor, as well as the telephone number where relevant. The box should also be marked 'urgent, livestock' or something similar. It is best not to advertise that the package contains reptiles or it may be subject to unwelcome attention.

Quarantine

All new reptiles being added to a collection should undergo a period of quarantine to ensure that one does not introduce disease or parasites into the existing stock. The animals should be placed in simple cages, with the minimum of equipment, and kept under close observation for a period of not less than twenty-one days. If all is well after this time they can be introduced to the main collection. Quarantine cages should, preferably, be kept in a separate room to minimise the danger of parasitic infestation.

Inspection and Handling

On arrival, the new acquisitions should be given a thorough examination for signs of external parasites and other indications of ill health, which will be discussed later. Thereafter, it is good policy to inspect the reptiles thoroughly on a monthly basis to ensure all is well. With the exception of some of the boid and colubrid snakes, most reptiles object to being handled too frequently, and this should be avoided with breeding specimens as it may interfere with the natural processes. Methods of handling lizards and snakes will vary depending on the size and the aggressiveness of the species or individual. Many will quickly become tame and are easily handled, particularly if reared from young. Others remain aggressive all of their lives.

Handling a large, boisterous lizard—a rhinoceros iguana, *Cyclura cornuta*

Small Lizards Geckos and other small lizards, up to about 20cm (7¾in) in length, can be grasped gently, but firmly, by placing the hand over the body and restraining them in the neck region with the thumb and forefinger. Never pick lizards up by the tail as a number of them practise autotomy and will shed the tail at the slightest provocation. Many small lizards will attempt to bite on being picked up but they are too weak and the teeth too short to break the human skin.

Medium Sized Lizards Lizards in the middle range of size up to 50cm (19½in) should be grasped round the thoracic region of the body, with the thumb and forefinger around the neck to restrain the head and prevent biting. The forelimbs can be restrained by holding them between the fingers and the rear end of the body should be grasped with the other hand. Lizards in this size range are capable of giving painful bites but, with a few exceptions, are incapable of causing deep wounds and usually just break the skin. Such minor wounds can simply be wiped with antiseptic.

Large Lizards Those species in excess of 50cm (19½in), in particular, monitors, iguanids, and teiids, can give painful and deep bites as well as lacerations caused by the sharp claws. Such lizards may require two people to restrain them. They should be grasped firmly round the neck with one hand, round the waist with the other, and the reptile hugged to the body with the rear legs and tail restrained by the elbow. Needless to say, one should wear old clothes when handling reptiles in case of damage by the claws or soiling from the faecal matter of nervous specimens, which will void the contents of the cloaca when restrained.

Small Snakes Specimens up to about 40cm (15¾in) in length can be grasped around the neck with the thumb and forefinger, allowing the body to drape over the hand. Bites from small non-venomous snakes are negligible, consisting of very minor skin punctures which can be wiped with antiseptic.

Medium Sized Snakes Species up to 1.5m (5ft) require handling with both hands. If the snake is tame it can simply be lifted up about one-third and two-thirds down the body and draped over the arms, restraining it occasionally as it crawls about. Aggressive snakes should be secured by the neck — just behind the head — with one hand, supporting the body with the other. Particularly difficult specimens may require the use of snake handling equipment of the type described for venomous snakes.

The milk snake has one of widest distributions of any American snake. This specimen is the subspecies *Lampropeltis triangulum hondurensis*, from Central America

Large Snakes Specimens, usually boids, in excess of 1.5m (5ft) are capable of giving deep, lacerated bites and their powers of constriction should be treated with respect. Most boids, however, become remarkably tame after a few handling sessions and thereafter can be simply lifted by the body and draped around one's shoulders. Aggressive specimens should be handled by two people, one of whom should grip the snake firmly by the neck while the other prevents the tail and body from getting a constrictive hold.

Venomous Snakes

All venomous snakes should be treated with the utmost respect and they are certainly not recommended for the beginner. Anyone who handles venomous snakes should first have had plenty of practice handling aggressive non-venomous ones in order to get an idea of the sort of problems involved. It is also a good idea to serve a short apprenticeship with somebody who is experienced with such reptiles before obtaining any specimens. It is worth repeating here that the prospective keeper should familiarise himself with all rules, regulations and safety procedures.

In general, it can be said that viperids are easier to handle than elapids, but there are exceptions. Most viperids are fairly sluggish and cumbersome in movement (though they may have a lightning strike) and can be picked up with a snake hook. This consists of a piece of metal rod with a 'T' or 'L' shaped end. The hook is slipped under the centre of the snake's body and it is lifted up. With very large viperids, it may be necessary to use two snake hooks or a combination of hook and grab. Always ensure that the handle of the hook or grab used is longer than two-thirds the length of the snake, and always hold the snake well away from the body (and from other people).

Elapid snakes and rear-fanged colubrids should be handled with a snake grab. This consists of a long rod with a handle and control grip at one end and a cable controlled tong at the other. Such instruments as fruit or litter pickers can be converted to snake grabs, usually by cushioning the tongs with foam rubber to prevent injury to the snakes. Some companies make special snake grabs and information about these may be obtained through your herpetological society or your local zoo.

Should it become necessary to grasp a venomous snake in the hand, and this should only be for specific examination, medical treatment or venom extraction (milking), the head of the snake should be first pinned to the surface on which it is resting, using the 'T' end of the snake stick. This should be done firmly, but not applying too much pressure which would cause injury. Having secured the snake with the stick, the other hand is used to grasp the snake with thumb and forefinger immediately behind the head, ensuring that one has not left enough neck for the snake to turn its head round and bite. The snake stick can then be discarded and the free hand used to restrain the snake's body. The technique is one which can never be

(left) Handling a large, potentially aggressive snake—a *boa constrictor*; (right) Using a grab stick to restrain a venomous snake—a puff adder, *Bitis arietans*

accurately described in writing and, unfortunately, the only way to gain experience is to try it out. A second person should always be around in case of emergency or to give help with difficult specimens. The appropriate antivenene vaccine should be available, preferably lodged at the surgery of the local general practitioner or at the local hospital, where expert medical treatment will be available in case of accidents.

Nutrition

All animals require a balanced diet the constituents of which include protein (for growth, repair and replacement of body tissue), carbohydrate (for energy requirements), fats (for energy requirements and storage), minerals, particularly calcium and phosphorus (for bone growth and repair, proper function of the cell membranes and the buffering of body fluids), vitamins (various functions – see nutritional diseases) and finally water (the elixir of life).

Until recently, the nutritional requirements of captive reptiles have been mainly speculative and based on our knowledge of the husbandry of domestic or agricultural animals. In particular, the protein metabolism of domestic fowl and reptiles bears a certain similarity, but a major variant is that reptiles do not have the high energy requirement of fowl to maintain a constant high body temperature. However, it can be assumed that each species of reptile has its own nutritional requirements based on the type and variety of food items obtainable in the specific habitat. Some attempt should be made to find out what the basic diet is and provide as near as possible to this in the captive environment. Unfortunately, it is nearly always necessary to provide substitute food in the terrarium. For example, nobody could be expected to provide the variety of food consumed by an insectivorous lizard in the wild; nor could one hope to provide specialist feeders, such as some tree snakes, with a continuous supply of tree frogs or geckos. Therefore, compromise has to be made but in so doing one must ensure that the captives' nutritional requirements are adequately met.

Food Items

Lizards and snakes require a variety of food items and one of the considerations to be borne in mind when selecting a particular species is whether one is in the position to obtain, or afford, a regular supply of the appropriate food. Lizards may be carnivorous, herbivorous or omnivorous, snakes are invariably carnivorous. The feeding of individual species is covered in Chapters 6 and 7 but the following gives details of the more readily available items.

9 Ocellated skink, *Chalcides ocellatus*, a docile terrarium inmate. This specimen came from Sicily.

10 Blue-tongued skink, *Tiliqua scincoides*. This Australian species is much sought after for the terrarium

11 Girdled lizard, *Cordylus giganteus*. The illustration shows a newly-born juvenile, which is much more colourful than the adults

12 Algerian sand racer, *Psammodromus algirus*. An extremely agile lacertid, that requires similar husbandry to that of the spiny-footed lizard

Foliage Sweepings Many small lizards and hatchlings require a constant supply of tiny insects and other invertebrates and in tropical countries, or in the temperate summer, large numbers of suitable items can be obtained by using a sweep net amongst foliage. A fine mesh net, similar to a butterfly net, is swept through long grass and the foliage of trees and shrubs to produce a veritable pot-pourri of flies, moths, beetles, bugs, caterpillars, aphids, grasshoppers, spiders and other such items which will be eagerly taken by the reptiles. Such sweepings should be kept in glass jars and fed sparingly to the reptiles after being size-graded. Only as much as can be eaten in a short period should be given, otherwise one will soon have a house full of unwanted guests! During the temperate winter, such sweepings will not be available and one will have to rely on the limited number of feed species available from the specialist suppliers. Some of these are quite easy to breed in the home, but if one has a good inexpensive and reliable supplier it is often more economical to purchase regular supplies rather than spend the extra time and money on home breeding projects.

Mealworms These most famous of all livefoods for many captive animals are the larvae of the flour beetle, *Tenebrio molitor*. Said by some to be unsuitable in too great a quantity, the mealworm is a nutritious item although calcium may have to be added in supplement form. This can be accomplished by adding a powdered vitamin/mineral supplement to the culture. Mealworms should be kept in shallow trays with about 5cm (2in) depth of bran covered with a piece of sacking. One or two pieces of carrot or apple placed on the sacking will provide enough moisture. Some of the mealworms should be allowed to pupate and mature into adult beetles to ensure an ongoing supply of various sized worms, from hatchlings to large sized worms, pupae and beetles — all of which will be accepted by many insectivorous lizard species. At intervals of two or three months a new culture should be started with fresh bran, and after as many mealworms as possible have been sifted from the old culture, it should be discarded. The danger of mealworms is that as they are so readily available they tend to be fed as a staple, unvaried diet. They should, in fact, be regarded as a standby in the absence of more varied food, and given sparingly when other food is available.

Crickets Various species of cricket are available from specialist suppliers, the most usual being *Gryllus bimaculatus*. These are nutritious insects taken greedily by many insectivorous reptiles. They may be kept in small glass containers with rolls of corrugated cardboard as hiding places. A small tube of water, with cotton wool plugged into the end, will provide moisture for the insects to drink and they may be fed on greenfood, carrots and a little fruit, which must be replaced at regular intervals to avoid rotting. Some dryfood, such as bran or rolled oats, may also be given. The container should be kept at about 30°C and the crickets should then breed prolifically. The various sizes of the nymphs and the adults provide a range of food for various sized reptiles.

Locusts The species of locust usually available is *Locusta migratoria* which is another nutritious food. These insects require a glass fronted cage with adequate ventilation and a day temperature of about 33°C, falling to 27°C at night. They are fed on grass stalks which are standing in a glass of water — and which is packed around the rim with cotton wool to prevent the insects falling in and drowning. The wet cotton wool will also provide drinking water. Locusts are more difficult to breed than crickets and require tubes of sand let into the cage floor in which the females can lay their eggs. For the person with only a few insectivorous reptiles, it is usually more economical to purchase a regular supply of locusts than to attempt the difficult and time consuming task of breeding them.

Flies Several species of fly, including the housefly, *Musca domestica*, the lesser housefly, *Fannia canicularis*, the bluebottle, *Calliophora vomitoria*, and the greenbottle, *Lucilia caesar* are all suitable as food. The adults are usually accepted more readily than the larvae, particularly those of *Calliophora* which are the maggots or gentles available as fishing bait. Such maggots possess a tough leathery skin and will often pass through a reptile's system undigested. However, these maggots can be allowed to pupate and metamorphose into adult flies. The full grown maggots are placed in clean bran or sawdust, contained in a small metal or plastic box, with holes in the lid large enough for the adult flies to emerge from when they hatch. The box is placed inside the terrarium and the inmates will soon learn the source of food and wait expectantly for the flies to emerge. One way to obtain plenty of flies is to use a fly trap. This consists of a boxlike frame covered in small-gauge mesh and a solid floor with a 5cm (2in) diameter hole in the centre. Over the hole is placed a mesh or transparent plastic funnel. The flytrap is placed in a sunny position outside over a piece of strong smelling bait (fish is especially effective) balanced on four stones so that the base of the trap is not more than 1cm (½in) from the floor. The flies will crawl under the trap to get at the bait, but when they leave it they will go for the nearest source of light through the funnel and into the trap. A muslin sleeve can be set into the side of the trap so that the flies can be caught up in small containers.

Fruit Flies These tiny flies are almost essential if one is to satisfactorily raise the hatchlings of geckos and other small insectivorous lizards. Fruit flies of *Drosophila* species have long been used by the geneticist for research, mainly due to the speed with which they reproduce. Such ability can also be taken advantage of by the breeder of small reptiles who requires a steady supply of suitably sized insects. *Drosophila* species are normally cultured in a specially made medium consisting of the following ingredients dissolved in 1 litre ($1\frac{3}{4}$pt) of boiling water: 7g ($\frac{1}{4}$oz) agar, 70g ($2\frac{1}{2}$oz) sugar and 120g (4oz) of ground maize. The solution is used to half fill a number of small bottles and is allowed to set. A small quantity of dried yeast is mixed with water and added to the surface of the medium and finally a small piece of fruit is added. The open bottles are placed in an area likely to attract fruit flies (near a compost heap or somewhere similar) and it will not be long before a number of flies are attracted into the bottles. The necks are plugged loosely with cotton wool to prevent their escape and they will soon breed, laying their eggs on the surface of the medium. It is possible to keep several broods rotating in a number of bottles — small amounts of the medium containing larvae are simply added to the next medium. When sufficient flies are hatching from a particular culture the cotton wool plug is removed and replaced by a lid with a hole in the centre, just large enough for the flies to emerge. The whole bottle may then be placed in the terrarium and the emerging flies will be eagerly snapped up by the waiting reptiles.

Other Insects Many other insect species may be purchased, collected or bred, and it is up to the individual how much effort he is prepared to devote to giving his reptiles a variety. Other insects which may be obtained as cultures include wax moths, flour moths, grain beetles, weevils, cockroaches, and even stick insects. Many of these are potentially excellent foods for small reptiles and the supplier will usually give information on their culture when they are purchased.

Earthworms The common earthworm, *Lumbricus terrestris*, is an extremely nutritious item in the diet of many captive reptiles, although unfortunately, some species will not take them. However, some lizards, garter snakes and burrowing snakes will take them readily, and as they are usually easy to obtain they should not be ignored. Anyone with a garden can collect earthworms on a regular basis. A layer of dead leaves about 3–5cm ($1\frac{1}{2}$in thick) is placed in a secluded corner of the garden and covered with a piece of damp sacking, which is regularly sprayed with water during dry weather. Many worms can be collected daily for a period of two or three weeks by lifting the sack and sifting among the leaves. As soon as the area becomes sparse in worms, a new trap can be set-up in another part of the garden. Worms should not be collected from compost, or manure heaps, as the bodies may sometimes contain toxic substances.

Fish Many reptiles will take either live or dead fish. Small tropical fish such as guppies, which breed prolifically, are a good standby for watersnakes, garter snakes and some lizards. Even frog and gecko eaters, such as long nosed tree snakes, can be trained to take live guppies by offering them in a shallow container of water so that the fish flop about. Some snakes can be trained to take strips of dead fish but this should be used sparingly, and always given with a vitamin/mineral supplement. It is always preferable to use fresh water fish rather than marine varieties as the latter are likely to contain the anti-vitamin, thiaminase, which breaks down vitamin B_1 and will cause Hypovitaminosis B_1. A good source of fish as a food item is the local trout farm where it is possible to obtain various sizes from fry upwards. Trout require cold, highly oxygenated water if they are to stay alive for any appreciable time, so unless such facilities are available it is wise to purchase only that quantity which can be consumed fairly soon. Goldfish are also a good standby and if one has a breeder in the area it may be possible to obtain rejects at a very reasonable price. Many breeders cull out fish at regular intervals so it may even be possible to obtain these free. One can always freeze a number of fish for future use but these must be thoroughly thawed out before being fed to the reptiles.

Day Old Chicks These may be obtained cheaply from hatcheries either alive or dead. Some companies supply large quantities of deep frozen birds which can be thawed out and fed to the reptiles as necessary. It may be a good idea to obtain young chicks and let them grow up to various sizes suitable for feeding to larger boids. Chicks which are a few days old and have started to grow are more nutritious than hatchlings.

Mice and Rats Laboratory rats and mice are the staple diet of many captive rodent-eating lizards and snakes. Wild rodents should be avoided as they may transmit diseases or parasites to the reptiles. It is up to the individual whether one is prepared to breed sufficient quantities of rodents for the reptiles, or to purchase them as required. Like day old chicks, mice and rats may be obtained deep frozen in bulk from specialist suppliers.

Vegetable Foods Many lizard species, iguanids in particular, are herbivorous or omnivorous and take varying amounts of vegetable matter in their food. Even some generally carnivorous species will occasionally take soft fruit or grated vegetables. All of the usual salad items are suitable and there are a number of wild plants which can be used to make as great a variety as possible for the reptiles. Lettuce, tomatoes, cucumber, peppers, carrots (grated), cabbage (finely shredded), bananas, apples, pears, oranges, grapes, boiled potatoes and various other household fruit and vegetables can be utilised. Some of the smaller iguanids may be fussy feeders and a whole range of foods may have to be experimented with before regular feeding commences. Quite often tinned fruit, such as pineapple or peaches, will initially tempt a difficult specimen, and even such items as tinned peas or baked beans may provide the necessary feeding stimulus. Species such as the desert iguana, *Dipsosaurus dorsalis*, which feed on the pungent leaves of the creosote bush in the wild, may often be tempted with plants from the herb garden such as rosemary or catmint.

Other Foods Many carnivorous lizards may be given minced, lean meat, and heart or liver; canned dog or cat food is also an excellent standby item. Eggs are also very useful and some larger lizards will eat these whole. With smaller lizards, eggs can be mixed with the meat and other items, the shell being crushed and included.

Vitamin/Mineral Supplements Snakes which take whole animal prey rarely require additional supplements to their normal food but many insectivorous and herbivorous lizards, particularly those species which bask in the sun, will require an additional supplement. It is considered that those proprietary brands of vitamin/mineral supplements available in powder form are best, as they can simply be added to the food. The addition of fluid supplements to the drinking water is a hit and miss affair, as many species from arid zones rarely drink. General purpose vitamin/mineral supplements may be obtained from pharmacists or pet stores, the former are primarily for human use, the latter for domestic animals, but most brands are perfectly suitable for reptiles. One should ensure that a range of vitamins is available, as well as minerals in the form of calcium and phosphorus compounds in particular. A small amount of the powder sprinkled on the food about once per week should be adequate to provide the reptiles with all they need. Insects can be dusted with the powder before they are fed to the reptiles. One method of ensuring that hatching flies are coated with powder is to have a tube at the exit of the hatching container; a small amount of powder is applied to the inside of the tube and the insects will pick some of this up on their bodies as they leave.

Feeding Techniques In general, it can be said that the smaller the species the more often it will need to be fed. Small insectivorous lizards and all herbivorous lizards should be fed daily. Large carnivorous lizards should be fed about three times per week, small snakes about twice per week, medium sized snakes once per week, and with very large snakes once a fortnight should be adequate. It is difficult to lay down any hard and fast rules as to the amount of food to be given and a certain amount of experimentation will be necessary in order to arrive at a suitable routine. When insects are fed, only enough which can be consumed in a few minutes should be given; as soon as the reptiles stop actively pursuing them feeding should cease for twenty-four hours. Dead animal food, meat, eggs and certain fruit which remains uneaten, should be removed before it begins to putrefy — and this will happen fairly quickly in the warm terrarium environment.

It must be remembered that all snakes and many carnivorous lizards consume whole prey animals which they may capture alive or find in carrion form. The fur or feather and bone of the prey animals is an important part of the diet, and provides roughage as well as valuable calcium and other bone building compounds. Thus, the feeding of lean meat on its own is not a sufficient diet and must be supplemented with whole food animals as often as possible. With the exception of those species which feed principally on fish, snakes will not normally require additional supplements to their diet as they will presumably receive whole mice, rats or chicks. The question of whether such items should be given alive or dead to the snakes is one which raises much controversy. Most snakes and large carnivorous lizards will soon learn to take dead prey, particularly if it is moved about in front of their noses. It is best to do this with a stick to avoid getting one's fingers bitten. Occasionally, a stubborn snake will refuse to take anything but livefood, and in such a case there is little alternative than to give it what it requires, hoping that it will resort to taking dead food later. Careful watch should be made whenever livefood is given, and if the snake shows no interest in it, then it should be removed from the terrarium and returned to its own accommodation; it is not unknown for hungry rats or mice left in a cage with a uninterested snake to turn the tables and gnaw into the reptile's body! All livefood kept for feeding reptiles should be given adequate hygienic accommodation and provided with the necessary food, water and bedding. The temptation to neglect such animals just because they are snake food should be avoided; not only is it immoral, but it can lead to prosecution.

Sometimes snakes in particular will steadfastly refuse all food offered. Having ascertained that one is giving it the correct food and having tried various kinds of such, offered dead or alive, during the day or at night, it may eventually be necessary to resort to force feeding. Before doing this, however, ensure that the reptile is not suffering from any disease or condition which may contribute to it losing its appetite. Mouth rot (necrotic stomatitis), difficulties in sloughing, internal or external parasites and many other conditions may affect appetite, and treatment should precede or accompany force feeding.

There are two methods of force feeding which can be tried. One is to take a whole, dead prey animal of suitable size and, opening the snake's mouth by pulling at the loose skin below the jaw, introducing its head first into the mouth. Sometimes a snake will start swallowing of its own accord but if not, it will be necessary to work the prey animal into the snake's gullet and massage it down into the stomach. It may be possible to use something like the handle of a wooden spoon to gently push the prey home. The second, more effective method of force feeding is to liquidise the food animal and place it into a large syringe, to the nozzle of which is attached a rubber or plastic tube of suitable length. The author has found a large cake icer to be ideal for this method. The end of the tube is lubricated with glycerine or liquid paraffin (mineral oil) and gently pushed down the snake's gullet into the thoracic region. The contents of the syringe are then simply squeezed out. Some of the more difficult species have been kept for long periods by this method which seems to do them little harm, although it is a shame they cannot be persuaded to feed in the normal manner.

Hygiene

Good hygienic practices are important with any captive animals in order to minimise the risk of disease and maintain them in prime health. If reptiles are kept on absorbent paper this can be easily changed each time it is soiled. If kept on other forms of substrate, the faecal matter can be scooped out as it appears, using a small shovel or a large spoon. At intervals of approximately one month, all materials should be taken from the cage and either discarded to be replaced or scrubbed clean. The inside of the cage can be scrubbed out with warm soapy water followed by a weak solution of bleach and finally swilled out with clean water, before being dried and refurnished. Domestic disinfectants other than bleach should never be used.

Drinking and bathing water should always be scrupulously clean and changed very regularly because many species delight in defaecating in the water dish, particularly just after it has been cleaned out. The glass viewing panels of the terrarium should be crystal clear at all times; there is nothing which destroys the aesthetic effect more than having the viewing glass smeared with filth. All these chores will take a little time but will be worth the effort in the long run.

Disease

With regard to disease, prevention is always better than cure and this applies to reptiles just as much as to humans or other animals. New arrivals should be quarantined for a period before introduction to existing stock. Any reptiles which become diseased should be isolated immediately, preferably in a special hospital cage in a different room from the main collection. Veterinary advice should be sought at the first opportunity; in the last few years the veterinary profession has taken a more active interest in exotic pets, in particular the diseases of the lower vertebrates which had hitherto been neglected. There are now specialised vets who are prepared to give advice to the general veterinary practitioner through the appropriate veterinary associations.

Any cages which have contained sick animals must be thoroughly disinfected using domestic bleach (sodium hypochlorite) or formalin, ensuring that all parts of the cage, its surrounding area, utensils and furnishings are treated. Dead reptiles should preferably be sent for a post-mortem examination; there are a number of pathologists and institutions prepared to perform such examinations free of charge, or for a small fee, in the interests of science. If a reptile dies from a known disease, or if it is impractical to send it for post-mortem examination, it should be incinerated. All dead reptiles should be placed as soon as possible in polythene bags which should be tied at the neck. If it is likely to be some time before they reach the laboratory, they should be injected with formalin in several parts of the body including the thoracic and abdominal cavities, the fleshy part of the tail, and the legs in lizards.

Types of disease may be divided into two main categories, non-communicable and communicable. The former are conditions caused by such things as incorrect environmental conditions, inadequate diet, and mechanical injuries, none of which are transmitted from one animal to the next; the latter are diseases which are infectious, the causative organisms spreading from one animal to another by various means if not checked.

Non-communicable Diseases
Environmental Deficiencies As already discussed, optimum conditions for reptiles are those in which the captive environment resembles, as closely as possible, that found in the natural habitat. Factors such as incorrect temperature, humidity, and quality of light

will soon affect the captive reptiles causing loss of appetite and the subsequent consequences. Life support systems should therefore be inspected at regular intervals and adjusted as necessary.

Stress This is a problem associated mainly with newly captured reptiles. The trauma of being captured, transported, and placed in an alien environment can take a toll on the animals' health and resistance to disease. Newly arrived specimens should be treated with the utmost care and respect, and handled as little as possible. Sudden movements in front of the cage should be avoided. Being creatures of habit, lizards and snakes become accustomed to a particular environment and learn exactly where the various basking areas, hiding places, water containers and other furnishings are situated. Therefore, once the initial terrarium is set up it is bad policy to change the furnishings around each time the cage is cleaned out.

Nutritional Disturbances One of the most common causes of ill health in captive lizards, slightly less so in snakes, are deficiency diseases associated with an inadequate diet, usually being a dearth of one or more vitamins and minerals. The most common vitamin deficiency diseases are as follows.

Type	Symptoms	Treatment
Hypovitaminosis A	Eye disorders, swollen lids, blindness, loss of appetite, and lethargy.	More varied diet Addition of vitamin/ mineral supplements to foods. Injections of vitamin A (by vet) in severe cases.
Hypovitaminosis B_1 (thiamin deficiency)	Disorientation, loss of balance, and convulsions.	More varied diet (particularly in snakes receiving dead fish*)
Hypovitaminosis B_2 (riboflavin deficiency)	Paralysis of limbs.	More varied diet. Addition of vitamin/ mineral supplements to all foods.
Hypovitaminosis D (rickets)	Weakening of the bones, subsequent malformation due to inadequate, calcium/phosphorus assimilation.	Wide spectrum lighting (ultra-violet), sunlight, and vitamin D_3 supplement to diet.

* The flesh of many fish species (especially marine) contains the enzyme thiaminase, which destroys the B_1 vitamin (thiamin). Before being fed to snakes, fish should be heated at 80°C for about five minutes to destroy the enzyme.

The most serious mineral deficiency in captive reptiles, particularly insectivorous and herbivorous ones, seems to be an imbalance of calcium and phosphorus in the diet. The ratio of calcium and phosphorus compounds should ideally be between 1:1 and 2:1. Unfortunately, the more commonly available insect foods possess a Ca/P ratio of anything from 1:3 to 1:14. The ratio in mealworms can be improved by adding vitamin/mineral supplements directly to the medium in which the insects are kept. Alternatively, the insects can be shaken in a little vitamin/mineral powder directly before being fed to the reptiles.

Sloughing All lizards and snakes shed their skin at regular intervals, usually at a rate of four to eight times per annum depending on the species and age. Lizards' skin is normally sloughed in patches and sometimes may take several days for all of the old skin to loosen and fall off, but this normally takes place without mishap. In snakes, however, sloughing problems frequently arise where the reptiles are kept in too dry conditions or if they are suffering from an infestation of mite. Normal sloughing is usually preceded by a lack of lustre in the skin, a fading of colour, and a milkiness of the brill (eye spectacle) which indicates the lubricating fluid between the old and the new skin is being secreted. During this period snakes will not usually feed, but the slough seems to make little difference to the appetite of lizards. Within forty-eight hours of the first signs, sloughing should commence and be completed within a few hours. The snake will first rub its lips against some rough object, such as a stone or bark, in order to loosen the skin around the mouth. A healthy snake will then literally crawl out of its old skin, turning it inside out much in the manner of a lady removing her stocking, and emerge as a sleek, colourful improvement of its former self. In an unhealthy specimen the skin will break into pieces before it can be peeled wholesomely and dried pieces will stick to the body. This skin must not be allowed to remain as infection can rapidly set in under the pieces of old skin.

Sloughing problems are more predominant in snakes which normally require a humid environment. The affected reptile may be placed in a container of lukewarm water in such a way that it is completely submerged (but allowed to breathe, of course), and left to soak for a couple of hours. Quite often the dried skin will then soften and float away in the water. Any which does not come away spontaneously can usually be pulled off gently with the fingers. Occasionally, the eye spectacle is particularly stubborn and remains on the snake long after the remainder of the skin has gone. It is therefore advisable to examine the sloughed skin to ensure that old brill is there. Obstinate brills can be lubricated with liquid paraffin (mineral oil) over a period of two or three days when they can usually be lifted with the finger nail, taking great care not to damage the new brill beneath. On no account should metal forceps be used to do this. Another method is to wind a piece of adhesive tape, sticky side out, round the finger and to gently dab the brill in the hope that it will adhere to the tape.

Mechanical Injuries Wounds suffered as a result of mechanical injury, due to fighting, attempting to escape, striking against the vivarium glass, or other such activities are susceptible to infection and should be treated as soon as possible. Such wounds should be bathed with antiseptic solution on a daily basis until they start to heal. Deep wounds may require surgery performed by the veterinarian.

Communicable Diseases

Ectoparasites The most usual ectoparasites to be found on lizards and snakes are ticks and mites. The former may often be found attached to newly captured specimens. Usually about 5mm ($\frac{1}{4}$ in) in length, they fasten themselves with their piercing mouthparts to the reptiles' skin, usually between scales and on secluded parts of the body such as below the jaw, around the vent, or under the limbs at the joint with the body. They should not be pulled directly away from the skin or there will be a danger of leaving the mouthparts behind, which could cause secondary infection. They should be first dabbed with a little alcohol (methylated spirit, surgical spirit or even gin) to relax the mouthparts before being gently removed with forceps and destroyed.

Mites particularly of the genus *Ophionyssus* (snake mite), can be a serious problem in the terrarium if not checked in time. Large numbers of them can cause stress, anaemia, sloughing problems, loss of appetite and eventual death. There is also the secondary danger of the transmission of blood pathogenic organisms from one reptile to the other, as is the case with all blood sucking parasites. The mites, which are about the size of a pinhead, roughly globular in shape and normally dark brown in colour (taking on a reddish tinge when bloated with blood), may be seen moving rapidly over the reptile's body or inside the terrarium. A new infestation is often indicated by the appearance of tiny white specks of dust (droppings) on the skin of the reptiles. An excellent remedy for mite is the insecticidal strip, normally used as a fly killer. One brand, known as Vapona, is particularly effective and a small piece, about 1sq cm per 10 litre ($\frac{1}{5}$sq in per cu ft) of air space, should be suspended in the terrarium inside a perforated container so that the reptiles cannot touch it, for a period of not more than three days. All free moving mites will be destroyed by the vapours emanating from the strip. The treatment should be repeated after ten days to destroy any nymphs which hatch from eggs in the interim period. Insecticidal strips should not be left in the terrarium for longer periods, as there is evidence to suggest that prolonged exposure to the vapours of some products can be harmful to the reptiles.

Endoparasites These are organisms which live inside the reptiles, usually in the alimentary tract. The most usual types of endoparasites found in captive lizards and snakes are various species of roundworms and tapeworms. Whilst wild reptiles, more often than not, may play host to several species of helminth without any apparent disability, the stress of captivity may reduce normal resistance and trigger a massive increase in growth, or in the numbers of worms, causing anaemia and general malaise which, if untreated, may result in death. Signs of endoparasitic infection include loss of appetite, emaciation, and the presence of worms, their eggs or segments (of tapeworms) in the faeces. Routine microscopic examination of faeces samples (arranged by a vet) will give evidence of degree of infestation by egg counts. Treatment may be given via stomach tube in aquaeous suspension or, in the case of snakes, injected into the dead prey animal. Suitable treatments for roundworm include Piperazine adepate, Thiabendazole and Fenbendazole at 100mg/kg body weight. For tapeworm, Dichlorphen 180mg/kg, or Niclosamide 150mg/kg body weight may be given. The advice of a vet should be obtained before attempting treatment.

Protozoan Infections These include forms of enteritis caused by protozoa, notably *Entamoeba invadens*. Symptoms include general debilitation and watery, slimy faeces which can rapidly reach epidemic proportions in captive stock. Treatment with various drugs (as recommended by a vet) via stomach tube have proven effective. Strict disinfection measures must be taken to prevent further outbreaks.

Bacterial Infections Various bacterial infections may affect the captive reptile. Infective salmonellosis manifests itself in watery, often greenish, foul smelling faeces. Treatment with antibiotics often proves effective. Certain *Salmonella* strains have been known to be transmitted from captive reptiles to man (particularly in the case of terrapins) so the importance of personal hygiene when handling reptiles and their terraria cannot be overstressed. Bacterial infections of the skin often appears as abscesses or cysts and these may be opened under general anaesthetic by a vet, the cavity swabbed with Povidone-iodine and the wound sutured.

A particular problem in snakes is mouth-rot or necrotic stomatitis, which often occurs in newly captured specimens which strike repeatedly at the glass of the terrarium, causing local wounding in and around the mouth which is invaded by bacteria. In severe cases the inner mucous membranes of the jaw margins swell to such an extent that the mouth cannot be properly closed, the bone of the jaw may be affected and death will ensue. Treatment with Povidone-iodine is effective in early cases whilst those which are more advanced may require surgery under general anaesthetic followed by antibiotic treatment.

Respiratory infections may occur in which the reptiles experience difficulty in breathing, blocked nostrils and mucal discharge. Often these conditions may be alleviated by moving the reptile to warmer, drier, well ventilated accommodation. Serious cases will require administration of antibiotics by a vet.

Surgery

Recent advances in veterinary techniques have resulted in a better understanding of anaesthesia and surgery in captive reptiles. The amputation of infected limbs, removal of tumours, repair of wounds and various other surgical operations, including such outrageous things as hysterectomy, are becoming commonplace, thus saving the lives of reptiles which hitherto would have died or have to be euthanised.

Hibernation

The subject of hibernation is one which has only relatively recently been classed as important in regard to captive reptile husbandry. Many temperate reptiles are kept in captivity at constant high temperature year in, year out, which is completely alien to such non-adaptive animals. Temperate reptiles require seasonal changes in temperature and a photoperiod as well as a period of immobility during the winter months. This takes place in the wild when temperatures are not adequate to permit normal activity. There is evidence to suggest that hibernation plays an important part in bringing reptiles into seasonal reproductive activity which normally takes place shortly after hibernation.

A hibernating captive reptile may be boring as it will not be seen for several months in the year. However, an adequate compromise seems to be a short rest period at a low temperature. This can be achieved by first of all ensuring that the reptile is well fed and has built up enough body to be able to withstand a prolonged period of fasting. Then stop feeding, and gradually reduce the terrarium temperature on a daily basis over a period of about fourteen days, preferably in an unheated room (but one which is not subject to frost). The animals can then be placed in a ventilated container loosely packed with just damp sphagnum moss. Ice cream tubs, margarine containers, or plastic lunch boxes are ideal for reptiles of various sizes and each should be packed separately. The individual containers are then placed in an insulated box, lined with expanded polystyrene, and kept in a frost-free unheated outhouse at a temperature of 4–6°C for a period of six to eight weeks. The process is reversed after the rest period; a gradual increase to about 12–15°C whilst they are still in the containers, return to the terrarium and gradually increase the daytime temperature to 20–25°C, cooling to about 15°C at night. Such treatment will normally trigger a natural breeding response.

5· CAPTIVE BREEDING

The most satisfying aspect of captive herpetology is the encouragement of the animals to reproduce. It is only reptiles that are kept in optimum conditions which will even attempt to court and mate, and it is therefore essential to possess a knowledge of the animals' natural environments before breeding is contemplated.

Sexing

The most essential and obvious requirement for captive breeding is a male and a female of the species to be bred. With very few exceptions (one or two lizard species are suspected of practising parthenogenesis), reptiles perform courtship procedures involving elaborate interactions between one or more individuals of each sex. The ease with which reptiles are sexed by the herpetologist varies greatly from species to species and in some cases this can be very difficult. In general, lizards are easier to sex than snakes, and a greater or lesser degree of sexual dimorphism exists in most species. The males of many lizards are much more colourful than their drab mates, some taking on even brighter colours during periods of sexual or territorial excitement. Males are often smaller and more agile than females, may have longer and more tapering tails, and sometimes possess obvious secondary sexual characteristics. An example of the latter is the three horns of the male Jackson's chamaeleon, showing a marked contrast to the hornless female. Such differences have in the past confused herpetologists to the extent that males and females have been classified as different species. The males of many lizard species possess pre-anal or femoral pores, sometimes a combination of both; in females these are absent or negligible.

In snakes, sexual determination in most species is relatively more difficult. In some families the tail is longer and narrower in the males than in the females and the distance from the vent to the tail tip is greater in the former than in the latter. This difference is particularly marked in Viperidae and in some members of Boidae. Viperids of the genus *Bitis* are perhaps the easiest of all snakes to sex, the females possessing a short, sharply tapering tail — the male having a slender appendage four or five times longer. In most snake species the adult females are larger and more robust than the corresponding males, although, of course, this does not help when dealing with immature specimens. The possession of the hemipenes in the males of both lizards and snakes sometimes shows a marked swelling around the tail base just to the rear of the vent, although this is not always obviously apparent. Subcaudal scale counts are a fairly reliable method of sexing many species, the paired scales below the tail being greater in number in the males than in the females.

Snake sexing probes can now be obtained in various sizes from specialist suppliers

The most effective method available to the amateur herpetologist is the so-called 'sexing probe'. In normal circumstances the hemipenes of the males of both lizards and snakes lay inverted (inside-out) in the direction of the tail and directly behind the vent. By inserting a probe into either side of the vent it is possible to pass inside the inverted hemipenes for a distance several times greater than that possible in the females. The distance varies from species to species but it is normally possible to insert the probe for up to ten subcaudal scales in the male but never more than two or three in the female. Sexing probes may be obtained from the specialist supplier and usually come in sets of various sizes suitable for small and large species or individuals. They may be manufactured from stainless steel, or synthetic materials, and basically resemble knitting needles with a small ball at the pointed end. The ball should be lubricated before use with vaseline or liquid paraffin (mineral oil) and insertion should be carried out with great care, so as not to cause injury. If one probe does not slide in easily then a smaller gauge should be tried. With practice, the use of probes to sex lizards and snakes becomes easy.

Surgical sexing, or hormone investigation of faecal or blood samples is sometimes carried out in zoological gardens and research laboratories, but is usually beyond the reach of the home vivarium keeper. These are reliable methods, however, and should not be discounted if the means and facilities are available in the area. Information may be obtained from reptile curators or specialist veterinary surgeons.

Reproductive Cycles

The reproductive cycles of all reptiles are affected by environment and seasonal changes, and, unlike the higher vertebrates, they are

13 Green lizard, *Lacerta viridis* (left) and wall lizard, *Podarcis muralis*, seen in an outdoor reptiliary at Cotswold Wild Life Park

14 Ruin lizard, *Podarcis sicula*. There are many documented races of this species

15 Slow worm, *Anguis fragilis*; an ideal subject for the unheated terrarium

16 Glass snake, *Ophisaurus apodus*; a legless lizard. The eyelids and external ear openings can be clearly seen in the illustration

unable to adapt to climates alien to them. It is very important to be aware of the natural environments and climates of the species in question; the provision of 'seasonal changes' in the vivarium will greatly enhance the chances of successful breeding. Most reptile species breed once per annum after reaching maturity, and breeding condition is brought about by climatic conditions at certain times of the year. Temperate species, for example, will benefit from hibernation (even if assimilated for a short period), followed by a progressive increase in the photoperiod and temperature. Species from dry climates may still require changes in temperature and photoperiod even if not hibernated. Certain species may benefit from a period of aestivation, others from variations in humidity. Many tropical species time their egg laying to coincide with periods of high humidity in order to facilitate satisfactory development of the embryo. With a little experimentation with heaters, lamps, time switches, and humidifiers it is possible to produce a mini-climate suitable for the reproductive cycles of most species.

Courtship

The majority of reptiles are fairly solitary outside of the breeding season and it is a combination of the correct environmental conditions and a chance meeting with a member of the opposite sex that triggers the courtship response and ultimate mating. However, some species are semi-gregarious and there is evidence to suggest that territoriality plays an important part in reproduction. Many lizard species, agamids for example, live in colonies, maybe in a tree or a rocky outcrop, where the males are continually striving to gain 'top-dog' position. The strongest male usually adopts the highest point of altitude available and advertises his superiority with bright colours combined with bizarre body movements, head bobbing, dewlap extending or other activities varying from one species to the next. The dominant male will keep his eyes on the available females and chase off any rival males which attempt to challenge his superiority. Sometimes, changes in dominance will occur, giving other males the chance to mate with the females. Most lizards approach females with strange stances such as outstretched limbs, arched or twisted body and perhaps wriggling of the tail; all are hallmarks of a sexually excited male. Often the female will appear to have little interest in the goings on until grabbed by the male, usually in the neck region, when she will either submit to mating or fight him off depending on whether she is receptive. Having succeeded in securing a receptive female, the male will manœuvre his vent into apposition with hers in order to insert either of the hemipenes into her cloaca. Copulation may take anything from a few minutes to several hours depending on species and individuals. Mating can sometimes appear to be quite a violent affair but the reptiles should not be disturbed during copulation.

With some of the more solitary species, breeding success can often be attained by keeping the sexes separate during the greater part of the year, introducing females to males at breeding time. This is particularly true in some snake groups such as the boids when courtship in physiologically prepared specimens will commence almost immediately after introduction. In the wild, several males may assemble at the vicinity of a receptive female and so-called 'combat rituals' take place. This takes the form of serpentine wrestling in which the males rear up and endeavour to force their adversary to the ground. The strongest male will eventually court and mate with the female. Courtship in snakes usually consists of the male approaching the female and moving over her in short, jerky movements, continually flickering the tongue in and out whilst so doing. Eventually, the tails and bodies are entwined and copulation will commence. In snakes this often takes several hours. In some cases the female will crawl about during copulation dragging the male by his hemipenes and occasionally causing minor injuries. Small amounts of blood left on the substrate after mating should give no cause for concern as such injuries usually heal up without mishap.

Failure in breeding a pair of snakes can often be overcome by introducing a second, or even a third, male, when combat procedures will produce the necessary mating response. In such cases, however, a close watch should be kept on the group as large pythons in particular have been known to cause deep wounds to their adversaries during ritual combat. Such wounds normally require veterinary treatment; the use of antibiotics and sutures normally results in a scarred but healthy specimen.

Gravid Females

All reptiles are either oviparous, ie the mother lays eggs containing poorly developed embryos, with a large supply of yolk; or ovoviviparous, ie the embryos develop full term within the mother, although making no apparent contact with maternal tissues for the purpose of nutrition. In simple terms the two groups can be described as egglayers and livebearers although in the latter case the embryos still develop inside an egg-sac which breaks at birth or shortly afterwards. A female reptile containing fertilised eggs is said to be gravid regardless of whether she is an egglayer or livebearer. The term pregnant should be reserved for marsupial and placental mammals and not be applied to reptiles.

The period of gravidity varies from species to species and may

take from thirty to sixty days in oviparous species and up to a
hundred days or more in those which are ovo-viviparous. In an
advanced state, gravid females take on a plump appearance and the
outline of the eggs can be seen as a series of bulges on either side of
the abdomen. At this stage they may refuse to feed until egglaying
or birth occurs; this is quite a natural event and should give no cause
for concern. It is advisable to refrain from handling gravid females
unless it becomes absolutely necessary, as undue disturbance may
affect the satisfactory development of the embryos. During this time
it is essential to check that the heating systems within the vivarium
are working correctly, as gravid females require extra basking time
to ensure optimum conditions for the developing young.

Egglaying and Birth

Egglaying or oviposition in ovo-viviparous species usually takes place
in a spot selected specially by the female as that most likely to
provide ideal conditions for the development of the embryos. The
correct heat and humidity seem to be the two major factors for
normal development. Recent research has shown that temperature
can determine the sex of some species; optimum temperatures producing a mixture of sexes but deviations slightly above or below the
optimum resulting predominantly in one sex or the other. In the
wild, the gravid female will have a wide range of prospective laying
sites and will sometimes spend several days searching for the ideal

Indian python, *Python molurus bivittatus*, laying eggs. These are roughly the size of
goose eggs (*Neier, Reptilianzoo Neier, Austria*)

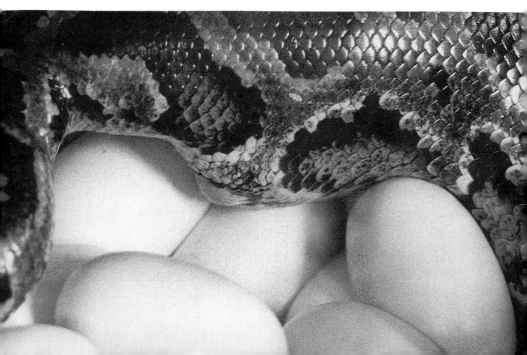

Glass snake, *Ophisaurus apodus*. This female is seen protecting her eggs in a sandy burrow found under a flat stone (*B. Langerwerf*)

spot. Most lizard species excavate a hole in an area exposed to the sun to ensure correct incubation temperatures; the depth of the hole will depend on the species and to some extent on the prevailing climate. The eggs are laid in the hole and carefully covered to avoid detection by predators. Some species will void the fluid contents of the cloaca over the eggs or on the excavated soil, probably to supply extra humidity as well as added compaction to the earth covering the eggs. Certain lizards, especially geckos, will lay their adhesive eggs on vertical surfaces, usually concealed inside hollow branches, in cracks behind bark or in cavities amongst rocks or stones. Such eggs laid on the walls of the vivarium, or on the furnishings, should be left in position as attempts to remove them will result in the brittle shell being broken. For protection, a small plastic container may be taped in position over the eggs. A small piece of moistened cotton wool can be kept in the base of the container — but not touching the eggs — for those species requiring humid conditions.

Snakes tend to lay their eggs in loose soil, in compost and manure heaps, in decaying vegetation or under logs and stones. Termite mounds are a favourite nesting site for many tropical species. Temperate species usually require a heat source additional to that supplied by the sun; for example, a favourite nesting site for the European grass snake, *Natrix natrix*, is the farmyard manure heap. In the vivarium, the choice of nesting sites is limited and it is therefore up to the keeper to ensure that one or more suitable areas are provided.

For small lizards, a container of slightly moistened clean sand can be placed in close proximity to a heat source. An ice-cream or margarine tub is ideal and a few rocks can be piled around it so that the lizards can gain easy access to the tub. For larger lizards, such as green iguanas or monitors, it is difficult to supply nesting areas of adequate size unless a great deal of room is available. Many species will not be happy with whatever facilities have been supplied and will end up laying their eggs haphazardly about the substrate or even in the water dish. Provided the eggs are collected up and placed in an incubator with a minimum of delay, it is usually possible to save them.

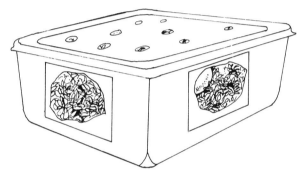

A simple egg laying chamber for snakes can be made from an ice-cream tub. One or two entrance-exit holes are made, and the box is filled with loosely packed sphagnum moss. Also useful as a hide box for some species

Snakes should be provided with one or more egglaying chambers and these can be made easily from margarine tubs with a hole cut in the side just large enough for the snake to gain entry. The tub should be loosely filled with slightly damp sphagnum moss and many snakes will be content with this arrangement. All eggs laid in the vivarium should be removed for artificial incubation, with the exception of the hard-shelled, adhesive gecko eggs, and those laid by pythons which should be allowed to incubate their own eggs.

Ovo-viviparous species are non-selective and will give birth wherever they happen to be at the time. The young are brought forth encased in a transparent membrane which will break shortly before, during, or slightly after birth. Occasionally the membrane will not break for a considerable time and, as the surface dries out, the young will find it increasingly difficult to escape. In such cases, after allowing nature to take its course for as long as possible, the membrane may be gently snipped open with a pair of sharp scissors, taking care not to injure the hatchling. In most cases the youngsters will be active immediately and will seek out hiding or basking places.

After giving birth, female lizards and snakes show no maternal interest in their offspring; indeed, they may even regard them as a tasty addition to the menu. It is best to remove the adult to a separate container after she has given birth, leaving the youngsters in peace to dry out and orientate themselves.

Incubation

In the past, the most difficult part of reptile breeding has been the satisfactory incubation of the eggs. It is only in the last two or three decades that a better understanding of the techniques required has brought the possibility of a reasonable degree of success to the serious herpetologist.

With the exception of the hard-shelled eggs of geckos, and those of incubating pythons, all eggs laid within the vivarium will stand a greater chance of hatching success if removed for artificial incubation. The eggs of most oviparous lizards and snakes have a soft, white leathery shell designed to absorb moisture from the incubation medium. Newly laid eggs often have a collapsed or dimpled appearance, but will soon fill out and become taut as moisture is absorbed. The eggs should be gently removed, and ideally kept the same way up to that which they were laid, then partially buried in an incubation medium contained in a plastic box. The eggs should preferably be arranged in rows and buried in hollows to about half their diameter, thus allowing for regular inspection without disturbance. Sometimes eggs may be laid in a clump and, if not discovered and separated before the surface mucus dries out, will adhere to each other. Attempts at separating such clumps should be avoided, otherwise one or more eggs may be damaged. The clump should be buried in such a way that all eggs have at least part of their surface visible for inspection.

Various methods of incubation have been recommended, ranging from placing the eggs on damp tissue which is changed daily, to burying eggs in sand, peat, sphagnum moss, or a whole range of other materials. By far the most satisfactory material, however, has proven to be vermiculite, a commercially available insulating material. It is sterile, retains moisture, and comes in various grades. A fine grade is suitable for incubation purposes and should be mixed with roughly its own weight of water. If sand is used it should be washed and sterilised, then partially dried out. Peat is best avoided due to acidity which may impair normal development of the embryos. The incubation box, which should have a few small ventilation holes in the lid, is placed in an incubator and kept within a range of 25–30°C. The nature of the incubator is of little importance provided the correct temperature range can be maintained, and many suc-

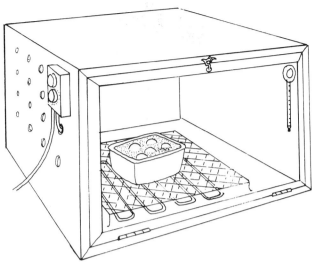

An easy to construct, home-made incubator, consisting of a glass-fronted wooden box. The eggs are incubated in a plastic box containing damp vermiculite and placed on a grid, over a thermostatically controlled heat pad or cable.

cessful hatchlings have occurred in the airing cupboard. However, it is fairly easy, and somewhat more professional, to make a simple incubator specially for hatching reptile eggs. A ventilated wooden box with a glass door on the front and heated by a simple light bulb, controlled by a thermostat, is all that is required. It is best to use a blue bulb in order to minimise the amount of light, which could have an adverse effect on the developing embryos. Alternatively, a heat cable or porcelain bulb can be used.

The eggs of most species will develop satisfactorily in the range of 25–30°C and variation within the range will do little harm: in fact, such variations will correspond to natural temperature fluctuations in the wild and should help produce a satisfactory ratio of males to females. As the eggs develop they will absorb moisture from the surrounding medium and increase in weight. Eggs which fail to absorb water are most probably infertile but should not be discarded until this is absolutely certain. Infertile eggs will soon become discoloured as the contents begin to putrefy and should be removed as soon as possible. Sometimes, mould may form on the surface of developing eggs, often causing no harm to the contents, but it is advisable to remove as much as possible with a fine, camel-hair brush. Although the eggs should be inspected daily they should be disturbed as little as possible, and should never be turned as one would the eggs of birds. After a week or so, fertile eggs will show well defined blood vessels through the shell, and if held up to the light the developing embryo will be seen as a dark shadow.

Incubation times vary from species to species and, to a certain extent, depend on the temperature; those in the lower range taking

A unique picture of an Indian python, *P. molurus bivittatus*, hatching from the egg. Note that the youngster is already testing the air with its sensory tongue (*Oxford and County Newspapers*)

longer than those in the higher. In most species the time averages between forty and sixty days and it can be very frustrating to the beginner to wait this amount of time. Patience is usually rewarded, however, and the day will arrive when the eggs show their first signs of hatching. As the fully developed embryo begins to absorb the remaining fluids within the egg, the shell may again collapse. At this time, the first slits will appear in the egg membrane as the young reptile uses its eggtooth to begin the hatching process. There is much variation in the amount of time taken to hatch; some lizards seem unable to leave the egg quickly enough and are scampering about within minutes of the first slit appearing. Certain snakes may take two or three days to emerge from the egg, sometimes sticking the head out but withdrawing it back into the safety of the shell at the slightest disturbance. It is a great temptation to help babies which appear to be taking a long time to hatch, but it must be remembered that it is a natural process which must normally be left to the animals themselves. The hatchlings will be absorbing the remaining contents of the yolk sac which is attached at the lower abdomen, as well as developing the use of the lung(s). On very rare occasions, weak hatchlings will become stuck to the egg shell as the albumen dries out; these can be released by gently bathing with a piece of cotton wool or lint, moistened with lukewarm water.

Rearing

The rearing of most snakes and lizards is not difficult, but there are a number of species which constitute a challenge, requiring a great deal of patience and time. Small insectivorous lizards, for example, will require a constant supply of minute livefood; many young snakes, particularly the specialist feeders, will require livefood of the type which they are used to in the wild. Nutrition, feeding techniques, and food items are discussed in Chapter 4 but there are certain points to be considered when dealing with youngsters.

Hatchlings should be removed from the incubation chamber as soon as they are free moving and detached from the egg shell. No attempt should be made to remove the yolk sac which will soon shrivel up and drop off. The tiny scar left on the belly will soon heal without treatment, although it would not do any harm to wipe it with a mild solution of medical antiseptic. It is best to house the young in small containers, preferably with no more than two or three specimens in each so that they are not overcrowded. Ice-cream tubs, or lunchboxes, with ventilation holes drilled in the lids are ideal for smaller species; small plastic or glass aquariums with secure ventilated lids are suitable for larger species. The containers may be housed in a heated room, or arranged inside a heated vivarium.

Ensure that the necessary requirements of temperature, lighting, and humidity are available for the species in question. Rearing containers should be furnished as simply as possible. Substrate material can consist of a sheet of absorbent paper; kitchen towels are ideal, but newspaper should be avoided as the ink may be detrimental to the animals' health. A small hiding box, a climbing branch, a rock if necessary, and a small dish of fresh water will suffice, as it will be necessary to inspect the progress of the reptiles at regular intervals.

Lizards may begin to feed almost immediately after hatching, provided the conditions are correct and the food acceptable. If one kind of food is not taken, try another and remember that once the animal is feeding on one kind of food, it can soon be trained to take other items. Snakes do not normally feed until after the first slough, which may be two or more days after hatching, or birth, whichever is the case. The frequency with which young reptiles will feed varies tremendously, even amongst the same species; consequently, some individuals will grow faster than others. A mistake which many beginners make is to overfeed those specimens which take food readily, which results in obese malformed reptiles which are not only useless for breeding, but will most probably die prematurely due to excessive fat build up in the internal organs. It is difficult to lay down hard and fast rules regarding the feeding of juvenile reptiles but, in general, small insectivorous lizards and small specialist feeding snakes should be fed as often as they will take food; larger snakes taking mice or chicks should be fed two or three times per week.

Ideally, specimens should be weighed regularly and the feeding strategy adjusted so that all reptiles from a particular hatching or litter increase in weight at a similar rate. Bear in mind that wild specimens have to hunt for food, and may sometimes go for quite long periods without getting any. Captive feeding is unnatural, so a compromise situation must be formulated. Many herpetologists have their own methods and it will sometimes pay to discuss tactics with fellow enthusiasts having experience with the species in question.

The rate at which reptiles reach sexual maturity again varies from species to species, and individual to individual, and may depend on such things as availability of food, temperature, and other climatic influences: for most species in captivity, an age of two to three years should be aimed at.

Breeding Records

Herpetoculture is a relatively new science and there are still many gaps in our knowledge regarding the reproduction and habits of many species. It is therefore highly recommended that records are kept of all relevant details (and perhaps those that may appear to be irrelevant at the time). Such records should be made available to other herpetologists through the society journals or by personal communication; it is only by combined effort and experience sharing that progress is made in any discipline. Individual ideas of record keeping will vary, but the author considers a daily diary and a card index are essential. Anyone possessing a home computer will find this invaluable in record keeping and will quickly be able to refer to items which occurred months, or even years, previously.

With the relatively few numbers of certain species in captivity, and the legislation which prevents collection of further specimens from the wild, it is obvious that an alarming amount of inbreeding will occur. It is only by the keeping of records and the co-operation of herpetologists that such inbreeding can be kept to a minimum by spreading the available genes as widely as possible through all captive stock. With some species, it would certainly be a good idea to have an international studbook, perhaps administered by a consortium of herpetological societies. With increasing success in the numbers of reptiles bred, it is inevitable that colour varieties of certain species will also become popular. Many species exhibit albinism or melanism and the time will come when bicoloured varieties are specially produced through selective breeding. Such an idea brings one into the realm of variety genetics, a discipline already widely practised by aviculturists and aquarists — so why not herpetoculturists too? The days when one may expect to obtain a Dutch ratsnake, an old English iguana, or a palomino python may not be too far away!

Breeding records are obviously the most important records to be kept and such data as mating behaviour, frequency of copulation, gestation and incubation periods should be noted. Individual clutch records should be kept, with such data as number, weight and size of eggs (length and breadth in mm, preferably measured with calipers), incubation temperatures, and times. Hatching behaviour should be noted and hatchlings should be weighed at regular intervals.

The sample clutch record has been given to illustrate how a simple card may be laid out. The amount of detail recorded on such a card will depend on the individual and can include such additional information as daily temperature and humidity levels, precise hatching times, results of bacterial analysis of the contents of dead in shell embryos, or any other points considered important. It is not necessary to mark the eggs themselves with numbers, as long as the position of the eggs in the incubation medium is not changed, the numbers can be marked on the lid of the chamber, or on a piece of paper stuck on the side of the incubator.

It is advisable to give each hatchling a number and/or a name; in the example given it has been assumed that the breeder's name is John Smith and the numbers of all snakes bred by him will bear the letters JS, followed by M or F for male or female. Each individual snake will have to be identifiable, of course, and in most species this can be achieved by taking notes of the markings on the head or body. Sketches of these will clearly be of great value.

CLUTCH RECORD | **Species** *Elaphe obsoleta lindheimeri* (Black Ratsnake)

Sire JSM 23 (Jason) | **Dam** JSF 6 (Barbara)
Date laid 2nd June 1984 | **Incubation temperture** 25–26°C

Egg No	Weight g	Length mm	Width mm	Incubation time (days)	Sex	Notes
1	15.9	49	18	65	f	
2	16.9	51	21	–	–	infertile
3	16.1	50	21	66	f	
4	17.3	59	20	66	m	
5	17.4	60	23	65	m	
6	17.2	61	21	66	m	
7	16.8	56	20	66	f	
8	16.7	56	20	–	–	died in shell

Note Egg no 2 developed mould on the tenth day and rapidly began to deteriorate. It was opened and found to be infertile. Egg no 8 developed mould on the 45th day and turned black by the 55th day. A partially developed dead embryo was found. Cause of death unknown.

6·LIZARDS OF THE WORLD

SUBORDER: Lacertilia

FAMILY: GEKKONIDAE – GECKOS

One of the larger families of lizards, the 600 or so species of gecko contained in 3 subfamilies and some 80 genera are distributed world-wide, throughout the warmer regions. Certain species, such as *Hemidactylus frenatus*, are almost cosmopolitan, having colonised suitable habitats by accidental or intentional introduction. Not all species, however, are so adaptable, some requiring the most balanced of micro-habitat. An estimated seventy-five per cent of gecko species are nocturnal as is evidenced in the structure of the eyes, the pupils of which contract to the narrowest vertical slit during the daylight hours. In the so-called day geckos the pupils are typically round. In all species the body is dorsoventrally flattened to a greater or lesser degree, the scales are granular, and in some species the skin is almost transparent. In many species the digits of the feet are typically adhesive, being provided with lamellae consisting of rows of tiny hooks which enable the animals to scuttle up apparently smooth vertical surfaces and even walk upside down.

Another notable speciality of the geckos is their ability to call, a phenomenon most probably related to territoriality. Calls range from a series of high pitched squeaks in some species, to sounds remarkably resembling the quacking of a duck or the barking of a dog in others. All species are carnivorous, usually living on small invertebrates though some of the larger forms will manage to overpower and swallow small vertebrates including frogs, other reptiles, nestling birds and even the young of small mammals. The teeth are pleurodont and the fleshy, protrusible tongue, with which it frequently cleans the brill of its lidless eyes, is notched rather than forked. Most species will breed readily in captivity given the correct conditions but the rearing of the young requires a steady supply of small insects.

Banded Desert Gecko *Coleonyx variegatus*
Subfamily: Eublepharinae
Length: 10–12cm (4½in)

Description This small gecko, like other members of the same family, departs from some of the typical gecko characteristics. The delicate looking digits are without lamellae and the eyelids are large and movable. The frail looking skin is yellowish-white, marked with a number of chestnut brown bands which extend into the bulky tail. The male is easily recognised by the spur-like protuberances on either side of the vent.

Range Western USA from California, through Arizona, Texas and northern Mexico.

Habitat and Habits A ground dwelling desert animal, often found amongst scree. It is crepuscular (active during twilight) and feeds on invertebrates. Mating takes place in late spring, with eggs being laid in June or July, and which take 30–40 days to hatch.

Housing A small, dry, heated terrarium or converted aquarium with medium sand and gravel substrate. A few rocks for hiding places and one or two cacti in pots will add an authentic touch.

Heating and Lighting Daytime air temperature of 22–28°C, allowed to fall to room temperature at night. Lighting is required for the benefit of plants.

Feeding Small invertebrates; mealworms in emergency. A water vessel is unnecessary but plants and rocks should be sprayed each morning. A vitamin/mineral supplement should be given weekly.

Hibernation Unnecessary, but a short winter rest period at room temperature with a cessation of feeding for 4–6 weeks will prove beneficial to breeding.

Community A single male is best kept with two or more females. Ensure that there are adequate hiding places for the number of animals kept.

Leopard Gecko *Eublepharis macularius*
Subfamily: Eublepharinae
Length: 18–21cm   (7–8in)

Description A robust, large headed gecko with movable eyelids. Skin is granular with numerous typical wartlike tubercles. Dark spots and blotches extend over the grey-buff body, into the short, broad tail. Males possess pre-anal pores.

Range South central Asia, from Iraq to north-west India.

Habitat and Habits Semi-desert, scrubland and rocky outcrops. Crepuscular, feeding on invertebrates. Adapts well to captivity and has been bred in large numbers in the laboratory. Females may lay up to five clutches of eggs per annum. Incubation period averages 60 days at 26–28°C.

Housing Similar to preceding species. One or two succulent plants can be installed.

The juvenile leopard gecko, *Eublepharus macularius* (above), is marked quite differently from the adult (below) and is sometimes mistaken for a different species

Heating and Lighting Similar to preceding species. Local ground temperature may reach 30°C. Lighting is necessary for plants only.
Hibernation As preceding species.
Community Males are territorial and aggressive. For best breeding results pairs should be kept singly and introduced for mating.

Tokay Gecko *Gekko gecko*
Subfamily: Gekkoninae
Length: 32cm (12½in)

Description One of the largest gecko species, the tokay is named after its loud, two-syllabled call. Possesses all typical gecko characteristics, including fused, transparent eyelids, vertical pupils and well developed digital lamellae. The robust body is blue-grey with numerous pink and light blue spots. The large head and eyes give it a fierce appearance, particularly when it opens its mouth in a typical threat gesture. Bites readily, and has vicelike grip, though the teeth are too small to do much damage.

Range South-east Asia.

Habitat and Habits Found mainly on old gnarled trees with many hiding places; sometimes in the walls and roofs of dwellings where they are encouraged due to their consumption of pests. Nocturnal and hunt invertebrates or small vertebrates. Breeds at any time of the year. Female lays two eggs attached to surface; eggs should be left in position if laid in terrarium and covered with small container.

Housing A tall vivarium containing gnarled tree branch and a few robust, potted plants. Pieces of tree bark attached to walls will provide controllable refuges.

Heating and Lighting Aquarium heater contained in a jar of water to raise temperature to 30°C and provide adequate humidity. Reduce to room temperature at night. Regular spraying of plants will be of benefit. Lighting subdued, and for benefit of plants only.

Feeding Variety of larger insects and even small mice. Will drink from small water container or take droplets from leaves. Vitamin/mineral supplement weekly.

Community Extremely aggressive and best housed in pairs only.

Colour Plate No jacket and 1.

Striped Leaf Gecko *Gonatodes vittatus*
Subfamily: Sphaerodactylinae
Length: 7–8cm (3in)

Description A small forest dweller. Marked sexual dimorphism, male being dark brown with vivid, black-bordered, white stripe extending along back into the tail; female light brown with much subdued dorsal stripe.

Range Trinidad; related species found throughout the West Indies and mainland Central and South America.

Habitat and Habits Very agile, but without digital lamellae. Female lays a single egg, but several clutches per annum. Diurnal (active during daylight).

Housing Tall, planted, tropical terrarium. Central tree branch with attached epiphytes can look most attractive. Substrate of washed shingle with a few potted plants.

Heating and Lighting Temperature in range 25–28°C, reduced at night. Broad spectrum fluorescent tubes for lighting; high humidity.

Community May be kept with other species of similar size and habit.

Males territorial. Related species include *Gonatodes ceciliae*, *G. humerilis*, *G. albogularis*, *G. concinnatus* and *Sphaerodactylus cinereus*.

Naked-fingered Gecko *Gymnodactylus kotschyi*
Subfamily: Gekkoninae
Length: 10cm (4in)

Description Possesses only partially developed, digital lamellae; however, these do not detract from its agility. The tips of the toes often bend upwards as the animal is resting. Light grey to brownish grey, lighter beneath, with a series of dark, chevronlike bands along the back and extending into the long, tapered tail.
Range Southern Europe, from Italy and through into south-west Asia.
Habitat and Habits Common in gardens and cultivated areas in the vicinity of walls. Mainly nocturnal, but sometimes basks in early morning sun.
Housing Tall, dry terrarium with piles of stones on peat and coarse sand substrate. Potted, dwarf, succulent plants placed among the stones will look attractive.
Heating and Lighting Small, white, infra-red lamp to raise daytime temperature to 25–28°C; minimum humidity; small container of water and occasional light spraying of plants.
Hibernation As recommended for *Coleonyx variegatus*.

House Gecko *Hemidactylus frenatus*
Subfamily: Gekkoninae
Length: 12–15cm (4¾–6in)

Description The common house gecko or chit-chat of the Far East. Typically gecko shaped with the usual attributes. Basic colour is sandy brown, with a number of darker blotches.
Range Originating in south-east Asia but has become cosmopolitan, due to its close relationship with man. It is found in many coastal areas throughout the tropics. In north-east Africa and Arabia, it is replaced by *H. flaviviridis*, which is similar in form but contains a greenish tinge in the coloration.
Habitat and Habits Found almost everywhere, from hollow trees to inside dwellings, where it may often be seen stalking insects on the walls and ceilings — frequently near to a domestic lamp. Nocturnal.
Housing A tall vivarium containing a few rocks and perhaps a couple of pieces of cork bark attached to the walls as controllable hiding places. One or two potted plants will help keep humidity levels up.
Heating and Lighting A small infra-red lamp or cable heater to bring daytime temperature to about 26°C. Lighting is necessary for the plants.

17 Southern alligator lizard, *Gerrhonotus multicarinatus*; an attractive species from California

18 Rough-necked monitor, *Varanus rudicollis*; an aggressive species — not suitable for the beginner

19 Papuan green tree python, *Chondropython viridis*; a popular snake that will require a large terrarium

20 Indian python, *Python molurus bivittatus*, the dark coloured Burmese race

Brook's gecko, *Hemidactylus brooki*, seen here perched on an apple, giving an indication of its size. One of several species in the genus requiring similar husbandry to *H. frenatus*

Feeding Small invertebrates; weekly vitamin/mineral supplement. Drinking water via daily spraying of the foliage, which will also aid humidity levels.
Community Territorial and aggressive; males should be kept singly.

Turkish Gecko *Hemidactylus turcicus*
Subfamily: Gekkoninae
Length: 10–11cm (4in)

Description Similar in appearance to *H. frenatus*, but with rows of black and white, wartlike protuberances along the body. The digital lamellae are wider than usual and resemble small discs. The colour is a mixture of reddish-brown and buff.
Range Mediterranean area. Has spread to foreign ports.
Habitat and Habits Common in and around dwellings, agricultural buildings and stone walls where it is mainly nocturnal.
Housing Similar to that described for *H. frenatus* but less humid. One or two potted plants may be added.
Heating and Lighting Heating cable or small infra-red lamp to bring daytime temperature up to 30°C. Cooler at night.
Feeding As for preceding species.

Hibernation A rest period at about 10–15°C, for 6–8 weeks is recommended.
Community Only with lizards of similar size and habit. Territorial.

Disc-tailed Gecko *Lygodactylus picturatus*
Subfamily: Gekkoninae
Length: 8–9cm (3¼in)

Description In addition to the normal gecko attributes, this species has an adhesive disc on the underside of the broadened tail tip. There is marked sexual dimorphism, the male having vivid, mustard-yellow stripes on the head and shoulders, merging into dull brown. Female is plain brown and the underside of both sexes is white.
Range East Africa from Kenya to Zimbabwe.
Habitat and Habits Found mainly in vicinity of trees, sometimes near dwellings. Occurs up to an altitude of 1,000m (3,250ft). Diurnal and crepescular.
Housing Tall terrarium with one or two branches and some cork bark. A potted, small palm or yucca may be used. A mixture of peat and coarse sand for substrate.
Heating and Lighting A small infra-red lamp or cable heater to raise daytime temperature to 25–27°C. Cooler at night. Broad spectrum fluorescent lighting; medium humidity.
Feeding Small invertebrates and a weekly vitamin/mineral supplement. Regular spraying of plants for drinking purposes; may also drink from shallow container.
Community Territorial, males are best kept singly.

Bibron's Gecko *Pachydactylus bibronii*
Subfamily: Gekkoninae
Length: 16cm (6¼in)

Description A small, robust gecko with wide lamellae reaching the tips the digits. The grey-brown body is marked with a number of marbled bands. Along the sides are a number of wartlike protuberances, particularly noticeable near the tail base.
Range Southern Africa.
Habitat and Habits Common in clefts and cavities of rocky outcrops and cliff faces. Also found in and around dwellings. Nocturnal.
Housing Similar to *Hemidactylus turcicus*.
Heating and Lighting Air temperature of 22–25°C; cable or infra-red heater. Lighting is necessary for plants; low humidity.
Feeding Small invertebrates and vitamin/mineral supplement. Regular spraying for droplets of water which the geckos will drink.
Community Territorial, males should be kept apart.

The charming green day geckos, with their bright red spots, soon settle down to terrarium life. This example of *Phelsuma laticauda*, from the Comoro Islands, is about to take a meal of honey

Day Geckos *Phelsuma* species
Subfamily: Gekkoninae
Length: 10–20cm (4–8in)

Description There are a number of species of day geckos which, due to their attractive green, red and white colouring, are popular as terrarium subjects. Most species are protected in their native habitats, but they are regularly bred in captivity and may become available. Unlike most geckos, the pupils of the eyes are round instead of vertical. Colours vary from bright to dull green and greenish-grey, with various red or orange spots, blotches or stripes.

Range Many species are found in the various islands and coastal areas of the Indian Ocean, for example *Phelsuma abboti* (NW Madagascar, Aldabra, Assumption), *P. cepediana* (Mauritius, Reunion), *P. dubia* (Madagascar, Comoros, Zanzibar), *P. laticauda* (Comoros, Nossi Be), *P. lineata* (Madagascar), *P. madagascariensis* (Madagascar, Sainte Marie, Seychelles), *P. mutabilis* (Madagascar), *P. quadriocellata* (Southern Madagascar), *P. serraticauda* (Madagascar), *P. vinsoni* (Mauritius).

Habitat and Habits Most species live on trees and foliage where they are extremely agile, scuttling about in search of insects. They will also lick the nectar from flowers. They are totally diurnal as their eye pupil would suggest.

Housing A tall, heated terrarium with adequate plants and climbing branches.

Heating and Lighting Infra-red heater for basking and aquarium heater in pot of water for humidity, which must be high. Both animals and plants will benefit from broad spectrum lighting.

Feeding Small invertebrates; fond of honey and sugar; vitamin/mineral supplement drops can be added to a sugar lump. Plants should be sprayed daily with water – the droplets providing the gecko's needs.

Community Territorial and aggressive. A mixture of species may tolerate each other.

European Leaf-toed Gecko *Phyllodactylus europaeus*
Subfamily: Gekkoninae
Length: 6–8cm (2½–3in)

Description The smallest European gecko. Long bodied and short limbed. Disc shaped adhesive pads at digital tips only. The colour is variable but usually grey-brown with yellowish marbling.

Range Southern Europe, mainly on the islands of Corsica and Sardinia.

Habitat and Habits Mainly nocturnal. Occurs in olive groves, scrubland or stone walls, where it hides in cavities during the day. Not usually found in dwellings.

Housing Small, tall terrarium with coarse sand and substrate. Decorate with gnarled tree branches and cork bark. Dwarf succulent plants may be added for aesthetic purposes.

Heating and Lighting Temperature 20–24°C provided by heat cable or small heat lamp which may be turned off at night. Low humidity.

Feeding Very small insects, spiders and foliage sweepings. Vitamin/-mineral supplement about once per week. Will drink from shallow container.

Hibernation 4–6 weeks at about 15°C.

Community Due to its small size, several specimens may be kept together – provided sufficient territorial space is available for the males.

Kuhl's Gecko *Ptychozoon kuhli*
Subfamily: Gekkoninae
Length: 15–18cm (6–7in)

Description An interesting species with webbed feet and a flap of skin down each side of the abdomen, joining the limbs. Further narrow frills occur at the sides of the head and along the tail. It is suspected

Kuhl's gecko, *Ptychozoon kuhli*

that these accessories are used to enable it to glide or parachute from trees when escaping from enemies, and also to play a part in camouflage. Ground colour is a mottled grey-brown with indistinct banding.

Range South-east Asia.

Habitat and Habits Lives on the bark of trees where it is excellently camouflaged. Often curls its tail laterally when at rest. Diurnal and nocturnal.

Housing A tall terrarium with several gnarled branches, cork bark and sand and peat substrate. One or two potted plants for decoration.

Heating and Lighting Cable heater or small aquarium heater in pot of water, temperature 25–28°C, cooler at night. Broad spectrum lamp for benefit of plants; high humidity.

Feeding Various invertebrates and calcium supplement (crushed cuttlefish bone); will drink droplets or from shallow container.

Community Best kept in single pairs; they breed readily in captivity.

Fan-fingered Gecko *Ptyodactylus hasselquistii*
Subfamily: Gekkoninae
Length: 13–15cm (5–6in)

Description As its common name implies, the adhesive digital lamellae are large and fan-shaped. The body is thin when compared to the large head. Upperside is sandy brown with a darker marbling. Two dark stripes run from each nostril to just behind the head. Underside is whitish.

Range Northern Africa and south-west Asia.

Habitat and Habits Rocky outcrops in desert areas. Found in old

Egyptian ruins and sometimes in dwellings. May be active day or night but remains in shadow.

Housing Tall dry terrarium with sandy substrate. Small piles of rocks or a mini wall for hiding places. A tree branch and a potted succulent plant may be added.

Heating and Lighting Infra-red heater. Daytime temperature 25–30°C turned off at night. Supplementary lighting is necessary for plants only.

Feeding Small invertebrates and vitamin/mineral supplement. Sprayed water two or three times per week.

Community Territorial, may be kept with other species of similar size and habit.

Moorish Gecko *Tarentola mauritanica*
Subfamily: Gekkoninae
Length: 14cm (5½in)

Description One of the most familiar geckos in Europe. A robust lizard with keeled scales, giving the skin a rough appearance. Colour is very variable ranging from black to sandy brown with lighter and darker marbling. Underside is whitish.

Range Mediterranean region and Canary Islands.

Habitat and Habits Very common around human habitations, but also found in walls, cliffs, olive groves and other such places. Often entering dwellings, they are nocturnal but may bask in early morning sun.

Housing Tall dry terrarium with gravel substrate and a pile of rocks, hollow branches or cork bark for hiding places. One or two potted succulent plants for decoration.

Heating and Lighting Infra-red lamp or cable heater. Temperature 24–30°C, cooler at night. Lighting for plants; morning sunlight appreciated by geckos.

Feeding Small invertebrates and vitamin/mineral supplement. Shallow water container.

Hibernation Rest period at 10–12°C for 4–6 weeks recommended.

Community Only to be kept with lizards of similar size. Territorial.

FAMILY: Night Lizards—Xantusidae

This small family, containing 3 genera and 6 species, is confined to Lower California, Central America and parts of the West Indies. Like most of the geckos, night lizards do not possess movable eyelids. The small dorsal scales are granular, those on the ventral surface being larger. Unlike the geckos, the tongue is very short and nonprotusable. They are all nocturnal and feed on small invertebrates, although one species, *Klauberina riversiana*, is said to include vegetation in its diet.

Yucca Night Lizard *Xantusia vigilis*
Family: Xantusidae
Length: 10cm (4in)

Description This small lizard has an elongated body and a long tapered tail. The legs are short and the digits narrow and clawed. The ground colour is greyish-brown with a number of darker spots and blotches.

Habitat and Habits A semi-desert animal which conceals itself amongst stones or the leaves of plants such as yuccas. Hunts small invertebrates at night.

Housing A dry, longitudinal desert terrarium with sand and shingle substrate and a few piles of stones. An artificial cliff face with controllable hiding places can be made. A potted yucca would be appropriate.

Heating and Lighting Up to 30°C air temperature from heat lamp or cable, cooler at night. Broad spectrum lighting for plants; low humidity.

Feeding Small invertebrates and vitamin/mineral supplement. Shallow water dish and occasional spraying of plants.

Community A number may be kept provided adequate territorial space is available. The granite night lizard, *Xantusia henshawi*, is a closely related species that may be kept in similar conditions.

FAMILY: Flap-footed Lizards—Pygopodidae

There are 7 genera and about 18 species in this family which is contained in Australia and New Guinea. The body is serpentine and there are no forelimbs. The hindlimbs resemble scaly flaps. The eyelids are fused and transparent, as in snakes and many geckos. The notched tongue is protrusible.

Burton's Snake Lizard *Lialis burtonis*
Family: Pygopodidae
Length: 25cm (10in)

Description A most unusual looking lizard, with a long pointed snout and poorly developed, flap-like hindlimbs. Colour is very variable throughout its range and it may be pale grey, cream, brown or even black. It can be spotted or striped with darker colours. It possesses external ear openings.

Range Almost the whole of Australia with the exception of the extreme south and Tasmania. A closely related species, *Lialis jicari*, occurs in New Guinea.

Habitat and Habits Ground dwelling, under logs and leaf litter and sometimes in low vegetation. Active by day and night.

Housing A low, woodland-type terrarium, longer than it is high. Substrate of a mixture of sand, peat and leaf litter. One or two dwarf potted plants.

Heating and Lighting Cable heater, aquarium heater or infra-red lamp. Air temperature 25°C, cooler at night. Local ground temperatures up to 30°C during the day. Broad spectrum lighting. Medium humidity but they can adapt to a range of these.

Feeding Mainly a lizard eater, but may be trained to take earthworms and other invertebrates. Vitamin/mineral supplement. Small water dish.

Community Best confined in pairs.

Flap-footed lizard, *Pygopus lepidopodus*

Common Scaly-foot *Pygopus lepidopodus*
Family: Pygopodidae
Length: 24cm (9in)

Description Another snakelike lizard but with prominent hindlimb flaps. The ear openings are prominent and the snout is rounded. The tail is relatively long, compared with the body, and breaks off easily. The regenerated tail is never as long or elegant as the original. Colour is variable, ranging through various shades of brown or grey.

Stripes may be present along the flanks. There are often dark bars on the sides of the face.

Range Southern parts of Australia but in the north it is replaced by *Pygopus nigriceps*.

Habitat and Habits May be found in wet, coastal woodland or inland, semi-arid scrub. Terrestrial, found amongst leaf litter or in low vegetation. Diurnal.

Housing As for *Lialis burtonis*.

Heating and Lighting As for *L. burtonis*.

Feeding Will take a range of invertebrates, including worms and small slugs. Weekly vitamin/mineral supplement. Shallow water container.

Community Best kept in single pairs.

FAMILY: Old World Burrowing Lizards—Dibamidae

This relatively unstudied family of lizards, found in south-east Asia and New Guinea, has 1 genus, *Dibamus*, and 3 species. The body is wormlike with girdles of scales. Limbs are absent, but in the male short, vestigeal stumps are apparent. The ear openings and the eyes are covered with skin. Due to their burrowing habits they are rarely kept in captivity so little is known of their husbandry. They probably feed on earthworms and other subterranean invertebrates.

FAMILY: Mexican Burrowing Lizard—Anelytropsidae

A single genus and a single species, *Anelytropsis*, superficially resembles the preceding family. It has a scaly, wormlike body and the eyes and ears are covered with skin. Found in central Mexico, there is little known of the captive husbandry of this lizard.

FAMILY: Iguanas—Iguanidae

The largest of the lizard families, Iguanidae contains about 60 genera and over 700 species. They show a remarkable diversity of form and habit and there are arboreal, terrestrial and even semi-marine forms (*Amblyrhynchus*). They mainly occur in the Americas from southern Canada almost to the tip of South America, but a few species exist in Fiji and Madagascar. Terrestrial forms are normally dorsoventrally flattened, whilst arboreal forms are laterally flattened. The limbs are well developed and most species possess a long tail. The teeth are pleurodont and the tongue is short and barely protrusible. There are

Marine iguana, *Amblyrhynchus cristatus*

desert and forest dwelling forms some of which are almost totally herbivorous, but most of the smaller species are insectivorous or at least omnivorous.

Many species are of bizarre shape, with crests and large dewlaps; colours, particularly in the males, are bright and varied, making them popular terrarium subjects. A number of species breed well in captivity if given the right conditions. Most lay soft-shelled eggs in excavations in the ground but some bear live young.

American Chamaeleon *Anolis carolinensis*
Family: Iguanidae
Length: 12–20cm (5–8in)

Description In spite of its common name, it has nothing to do with the family Chamaeleonidae, the only resemblance being that it is a lizard and has colour changing powers. The body and tail are long and slender, the head narrow and the snout pointed. Males are larger than females and possess extendable dewlaps of a bright pink colour, which they extend during territorial or sexual activity. Basic body colour is green, grey or brown which may rapidly change depending on the mood of the reptile. An unusual feature of the anole is its adhesive digital lamellae, somewhat similar to those possessed by geckos, which enable it to scuttle up smooth, vertical surfaces.
Range South-eastern USA from Carolina to Louisiana.

Habitat and Habits At home in trees, shrubs, on fences and sometimes even on the walls of houses. Avoids swampy areas. A diurnal, sun-loving lizard which is extremely active and a popular terrarium subject.

Housing A tall terrarium with plenty of climbing branches and a few potted, broad-leaved plants. A mixture of sand, peat and leaf litter is ideal as substrate.

Heating and Lighting Infra-red lamp to provide basking facilities. Air temperature 23–26°C, up to 30°C locally. Reduce to room temperature at night. Broad spectrum lighting; medium humidity.

Feeding Anoles prefer a great variety of small invertebrates and soon become bored if fed purely on mealworms or maggots. Regular vitamin/mineral supplement should be given and foliage sprayed for water droplets.

Hibernation A short rest period at room temperature (18–20°C) is recommended.

Community Males extremely territorial, but it is worth keeping at least two males in a large terrarium in order to observe displays. A close watch should be kept in case of injury (to the lizards). Tolerant to other similar sized species.

Large-headed Anole *Anolis cybotes*
Family: Iguanidae
Length: 20–22cm   (8–9in)

Description More sturdy in appearance than *A. carolinensis* and with a larger head. Basic colour is medium brown which changes to dark,

Green anole or American 'chamaeleon', *Anolis carolinensis*. This is one of the most popular subjects for the small, planted terrarium

The large-headed anole, *Anolis cybotes*. A bizarre species requiring humid conditions

nut brown when the animal is excited. The female has a darker stripe along the back than the male, with lighter cross bands.

Range The island of Hispaniola.

Habitat and Habits Unlike *A. carolinensis*, it lives mainly on the bark of trunks and branches. Diurnal, it is found in both forest and coffee or cocoa plantations.

Housing Similar to preceding species.

Heating and Lighting Similar to preceding species but temperature of 28–30°C.

Feeding Small invertebrates and vitamin/mineral supplement. Daily spray with water for droplets. Small, shallow, water dish may also be given.

Community Territorial.

Knight Anole *Anolis equestris*
Family: Iguanidae
Length: up to 35cm (14in)

Description One of the larger anoles, *A. equestris* is a robust lizard. Viewed from the side, the head is triangular with a rounded snout. Along the back is a short, poorly developed crest. Colours vary from green to brown, the underside ranging from yellowish to reddish. In the green phase, a blue band may be evident on the neck. The extended dewlap is yellowish-white with red markings.

Range Cuba; Florida (introduced).

Habitat and Habits Arboreal, found in thickly wooded areas where it is diurnal.

Housing Large, tall terrarium planted with tropical species. Epiphytes grown on a gnarled tree branch particularly effective.

Heating and Lighting Temperature up to 30°C but cooler at night. Infra-red lamp; an aquarium heater in the 'pond' will keep a reasonable humidity. Broad spectrum lighting.

Feeding Larger invertebrates, including beetles. Will also take newborn mice.

Community Aggressive, will eat smaller lizards. Best kept in pairs.

Giant Anole *Anolis ricordii*
Family: Iguanidae
Length: 45cm (17¾in)

Description The largest of the anoles, *A. ricordii* is a relatively quiet species, catching its prey by stealth rather than by chasing it. Similar in shape to *A. carolinensis*, but larger, it has a short, spiny crest. Basically green in colour with lighter blotches. The dewlap is very variable.

Range The island of Hispaniola.

Habitat and Habits Lives amongst the foliage in wooded areas, and is believed to eat nestling birds. Diurnal.

Housing A large, tall terrarium, decorated with tree branches and robust plants. Substrate of peat, sand and leaf litter.

Heating and Lighting As for preceding species. Small water container; high humidity.

Community Aggressive, best kept in single pairs.

The Cuban or knight anole, *Anolis equestris*, is one of the larger members of the genus

Brown Anole *Anolis sagrei*
Family: Iguanidae
Length: 15–18cm (6–7in)

Description A sturdy anole, with a short head and blunt snout. When excited, the male inflates his narrow crest as well as his dewlap, which is red bordered with yellowish-white. The basic colour is brown which will vary in shade, depending on the mood of the reptile.
Range Cuba; Florida (introduced).
Habitat and Habits More of a bark dweller than other anoles it is found in wooded areas where it is diurnal.
Housing As for *A. carolinensis.*
Heating and Lighting As for *A. carolinensis.* Temperature 24–26°C with medium humidity.
Feeding As for *A. carolinensis.*
Community Territorial.

Helmeted Basilisk *Basiliscus basiliscus*
Family: Iguanidae
Length: 75cm (29½in)

Description The iguanids of the genus *Basiliscus* are popular terrarium subjects due to their bizarre appearance. They possess quite remarkable dorsal crests which can be raised or lowered at will. They are slender, long-legged lizards with long, clawed digits. *B. basiliscus* may be olive green to olive brown in colour, with a yellowish underside. Broken darker bands cross the dorsal surface and there are lighter stripes along the sides of the head and body.
Range Central and South America from Panama to Colombia.
Habitat and Habits Like most basilisks it lives in trees near to water into which it will leap when disturbed. Runs on its long hind legs with such speed that it can 'walk' on the water surface for short distances. Diurnal.
Housing Very large, tall terrarium with adequate robust plants, tree branches and a spacious pond. Substrate of peat, loam, sand and leaf litter.
Heating and Lighting Temperature 24–30°C. Infra-red lamp; an aquarium heater in the pond. High humidity, enhanced by waterfall or aeration of pond water. Broad spectrum lighting.
Feeding Larger invertebrates, baby mice and regular vitamin/mineral supplements.
Community Aggressive, not recommended to be kept with smaller lizards.

The striped basilisk, *Basiliscus vittatus*, lacks the spectacular dorsal crest of some of its close relatives

Plumed Basilisk *Basiliscus plumifrons*
Family: Iguanidae
Length: 65cm (25½in)

Description Similar in shape to preceding species. There is a double crest on the head, a further one some 6cm (2¼in) high along the back, and a third one along half of the tail. This species is bright green in colour, with lighter blotches, merging into blue-green along the flanks. The underside is yellowish. Like other basilisks, the body is laterally flattened, thus demonstrating its arboreal habit.
Range Central America.
Habitat and Habits Tropical rainforest in the vicinity of open water where it is diurnal.
Housing As for *B. basiliscus*.
Heating and Lighting As for *B. basiliscus*.
Feeding As for *B. basiliscus*.
Community Only with lizards of similar size and habit. The striped basilisk, *B. vittatus*, is a related species from Central America that requires similar husbandry.
Colour Plate No: 2

Collared Lizard *Crotaphytus collaris*
Family: Iguanidae
Length: 30cm (12in)

Description Named after the black-and-white collar around the neck, this species is a large-headed, sturdy iguanid. The head is reddish-brown, the body yellowish-brown with whitish spots, changing into reddish-brown on the flanks. The male has a brightly coloured dewlap of blue or green.
Range Southern central to south-western USA and Mexico.
Habitat and Habits A true desert reptile. Lives in dry, stony areas. Diurnal.
Housing A low, desert terrarium with plenty of ground space with piles of rocks and an artificial cliff face. A dead, bleached tree branch as decoration with perhaps one or two potted cacti. Substrate of gravel or coarse sand.
Heating and Lighting Requires extremely hot basking areas (up to 40°C), and an air temperature of 25–32°C. High wattage, infra-red lamp fixed to heat basking area(s). Broad spectrum lighting, with ultra-violet, is essential.
Feeding Larger invertebrates, including beetles, cockroaches, and crickets; may take baby mice. Water should be supplied in shallow container.
Community Aggressive, will eat smaller lizards. Best kept as a pair.

Desert Iguana *Dipsosaurus dorsalis*
Family: Iguanidae
Length: 35cm (14in)

Description Small-headed with a long neck and a plump body, this species is a popular subject for the terrarium. A short crest runs the length of the back and into the tail. The body colour is light brown to cream, with little bands of dark brown and yellow spots. In strong sunlight the whole body colour lightens. The throat and underside are whitish.
Range South-western USA and Mexico.
Habitat and Habits A diurnal lizard with high temperature requirements. Climbs amongst desert vegetation. Hides in burrows at night or if disturbed.
Housing As for *Crotaphytus collaris*.
Heating and Lighting As for *Crotophytus collaris*.
Feeding Primarily herbivorous, but will take insects occasionally. Its natural food seems to be the foliage and flowers of desert plants. In captivity it seems to prefer various herbs with a pungent flavour.
Community A gentle lizard which will live peacefully with others of similar size and habit.

21 Reticulated python, *Python reticulatus*. Only experienced enthusiasts should contemplate keeping any of the larger boids — especially when they can attain the size of this species *Smetstow Wildlife Park, West Midlands*

22 Boa constrictor, *Boa constrictor*. Although a very popular snake with the terrarium keeper it tends to be less stable in temperament as it ages — a factor that should be considered if purchased when young

23 Green whip snake, *Coluber viridiflavus*; an aggressive but harmless European species

Green Iguana *Iguana iguana*
Family: Iguanidae
Length: 1.6m (5¼ft)

Description Probably the most well known and loved lizard, the green iguana is popular due to its bizarre appearance, gentle manner and an easy diet. It is a robust species, with a full elongate body and a spiny crest running from the nape down into the elegant whiplike tail. The male has an enlarged leathery dewlap, which is extended when he is excited. The basic colour is greenish-grey with darker bands but there is much variation. The young are bright green.
Range Central and South America.
Habitat and Habits Primarily a tree dweller, often near to rivers into which it will dive and hide if disturbed. Diurnal, it is an accomplished swimmer. Females migrate to communal nesting areas, where the eggs are buried some 30cm (12in) deep in the sandy ground.
Housing Requires extremely spacious accommodation. Anything less than 2m³ (2yd³) in volume is inadequate for adults. Requires large water container or pond and strong climbing branches. Planting is pointless as foliage will be eaten, or damaged by the heavy bodies. Gravel substrate.
Heating and Lighting Cable heater and infra-red lamps. Daytime temperature 25–30°C, reduced to 22–24°C at night. Broad spectrum lighting with ultra-violet; medium humidity and good ventilation.
Feeding A whole range of vegetables and fruit can be given, chopped into bite-sized pieces. Foliage of edible trees; various garden weeds and flowers will also be appreciated. Will sometimes take insects (mealworms or locusts). Regular vitamin/mineral supplement and adequate fresh water.
Community Good with other species. Adult males should be kept separate.
Colour plate No: 3.

Horned Toad *Phrynosoma cornutum*
Family: Iguanidae
Length: 12–15cm (4¾–6in)

Description This iguanid gets its common name from its squat, toad-like stature and by the numerous spines on the head and body. The spines on the head indeed resemble horns. The tail is short and sharply tapered from the plump body. The limbs are slender and seem not to match the heavy body. Colour is variable from reddish-brown to greyish-yellow, with a number of darker bands and blotches edged with lighter colours.
Range Central and south-western USA from Arkansas to Mexico.

Horned toad, *Phrynosoma* species

Habitat and Habits A diurnal, semi-desert resident. Found also on cultivated land. Feeds mainly on ants in the wild.

Housing A large, low terrarium with a deep substrate of coarse sand into which the lizards will burrow at night. A few rocks, a bleached tree root and a potted cactus for decoration.

Heating and Lighting Local basking temperature to 40°C is essential. Air temperature 25–28°C, cooler at night. Infra-red lamp or cable heater (local) and broad spectrum lighting is advisable.

Feeding Small invertebrates including ants. Vitamin/mineral supplement. Water may be given daily in a hollow in a rock.

Hibernation Short rest period at reduced temperature recommended.

Community Territorial, they are best kept in single pairs.

Granite Spiny Lizard *Sceloporus orcutti*
Family: Iguanidae
Length: 18cm (7in)

Description The keeled scales of this species and others in the genus, run to a point and give the appearance of spines. The body is fairly squat and the limbs well formed. The head is broad and the snout rounded. Colour is variable, ranging through various shades of brown. When basking, or when excited, a deep metallic blue colour appears on the belly and the back of the males. Females are more drab.

Range Western USA and Lower California.

Habitat and Habits A desert species, found amongst rocks and scrub. Diurnal.

Housing A low, desert type terrarium with gravel substrate, rocks, a log and potted cacti or succulents.

Heating and Lighting Local basking areas to 35°C. Air temperature 24–28°C, cooled to room temperature at night. Heat lamps or local

A rarely seen spiny lizard from Chile, this *Sceloporus* species requires similar husbandry to that of other members of the genus

cable heating; broad spectrum lighting; low humidity.
Feeding Small invertebrates and regular vitamin/mineral supplement. Shallow water dish.
Hibernation Short rest period at reduced temperature recommended.
Community A good community species with lizards of a similar size. Several other species such as the fence lizard, *S. undulatus*, the malachite spiny lizard, *S. malachitus*, and the western fence lizard, *S. occidentalis*, require similar husbandry.
Colour Plate No: 4.

Keel-tailed Lizard *Tropidurus torquatus*
Family: Iguanidae
Length: 15cm (6in)

Description This species is dorsoventrally flattened, with a broad head and a rounded snout. The long tail is decorated with a dorsal keel. The ground colour is grey with darker indistinct bands across the body. The flanks and limbs may show a series of light coloured blotches and spots.
Range Northern South America from Brazil to Venezuela.
Habitat and Habits A terrestrial, diurnal lizard, found in sandy scrubland.
Housing A low, semi-desert type terrarium with sand and gravel substrate. One or two rocks and logs for basking, climbing and hiding. A potted plant, of low or prostrate variety.
Heating and Lighting Infra-red lamp or cable heater (local); basking areas to 35°C; air temperature about 26°C, cooler at night.
Feeding Various invertebrates and vitamin/mineral supplement, shallow water dish.

Community Should only be kept with species of similar size and habit. The yellow-backed keel-tail, *Tropidurus semitaeniatus*, requires similar husbandry.

FAMILY: Agamids—Agamidae

The 35 genera and over 300 species of lizard in the family Agamidae comprise the old world equivalent of the Iguanidae, some species from both families showing remarkable similarity in form and habit. Like the Iguanidae, there are terrestrial, arboreal and semi-aquatic species which are found in a great range of habitat within the geographical regions of Africa, Asia, and Australia. The limbs are well developed and most species have a long tail which is used as a balance during locomotion. The teeth are pleurodont at the front, and acrodont at the rear, of the jaw. Some herbivorous species have almost incisor-like teeth at the front of the jaw (*Uromastyx*). Most are insectivorous or carnivorous.

Like the iguanids, many show bizarre form with crests, dewlaps and other expandable appendages, and the males are often brightly coloured. Many species will breed readily in captivity if given the correct conditions. Most species lay soft-shelled eggs in excavations in the ground.

Green Tree Lizard *Acanthosaura capra*
Family: Agamidae
Length: 28cm (11in)

Description A very agile arboreal species with the body laterally flattened, slender limbed and with a long tail. A spiny crest, particularly prominent in the neck region, runs the length of the body and into the tail base. Basic colour is bright green, which may be darkened when mood changes.
Range South-east Asia.
Habitat and Habits Found amongst the foliage of the tropical rain forest where it actively hunts invertebrate food. Diurnal.
Housing A tall terrarium with climbing branches and robust plants. Substrate of a mixture of sand, peat, loam and leaf litter.
Heating and Lighting Air temperature around 25°C, cooler at night. Basking area with infra-red lamp. Aquarium heater in water dish. Broad spectrum lighting.
Feeding Small invertebrates, vitamin/mineral supplement and water sprayed daily.
Community Should only be kept with lizards of similar size and habit. Males territorial.

Rainbow Lizard *Agama agama*
Family: Agamidae
Length: 40cm (16in)

Description The common agama of Africa. It is typically lizardlike in shape, with robust body, broad triangular head and wide jaw. Strong limbs and substantial tail. There is a small crest on the nape of the neck, and a spiny flap around the ear openings. Usual colour is reddish-brown, but when excited the males take on an amazing variety of hues, thus the common name. The head becomes orange red, parts of the back and limbs a bright blue, and yellow blotches appear on the flanks and tail. Basking females also show a variance in colour. Geographical races show distinct differences in colour distribution.
Range Central and western Africa.
Habitat and Habits It has a wide range of habitat from rocky to wooded areas and is common around human settlements, where it is encouraged as a pest controller, although some natives believe it to be poisonous. Diurnal.
Housing Requires a very large, terrestrial type terrarium with several branches and rocks. Only robust potted plants should be used. Substrate should be of gravel and coarse sand mixture.
Heating and Lighting Basking area to 45°C – air temperature to 35°C. Heat cable (local) and infra-red lamps; low humidity.
Feeding A wide range of invertebrates; baby mice. Small water container.
Community Males should be kept separate unless accommodation is very large. Other species of similar size and habitat may share peacefully.

Blue-throated Agama *Agama atricollis*
Family: Agamidae
Length: 25cm (10in)

Description Similar in shape to the preceding species though somewhat smaller. Ground colour is a greyish-brown with a number of whitish, yellow, and darker spots. The throat and parts of the head become bright blue when the animal is excited.
Range East Africa.
Habitat and Habits Diurnal, it is found mainly in savannah and open woodland where it stays in the neighbourhood of trees. Always runs to a tree when disturbed and disappears with great speed to the other side of the trunk.
Housing A tall terrarium with sand and gravel substrate. Adequate climbing branches, a few rocks and one or two robust potted plants.

Heating and Lighting Air temperature to 28°C though local basking surfaces may reach 35°C. Infra-red lamp and cable heater (local), turned off at night. Broad spectrum lighting; low humidity.

Feeding Small invertebrates – fond of bees and wasps. Regular vitamin/mineral supplement. Small water dish and occasional spraying will be appreciated.

Community Should only be kept with lizards of similar size and habit. Males are strongly territorial.

Desert Agama *Agama mutabilis*
Family: Agamidae
Length: 22cm (8½in)

Description One of the smaller species of agamid, the desert agama lacks the typical sturdy build of other species, being relatively slender. The dorsal scales are spiny in appearance and of irregular size. Basic colour is greyish to yellowish-brown, with a number of darker, blotchy, broken bands along the back. The eyelids are well developed to protect the eyes from the desert sand.

Range North Africa and Saudi Arabia.

Habitat and Habits It is at home in sand, on rocks, or in scrub areas. Extremely agile and wary, disappearing into crevices or burrowing into the sand at the first sign of danger. Diurnal.

Housing Low, desert type terrarium. Substrate of clean, dry river sand to 10cm (4in) depth. Pile of rocks and bleached tree root for decoration together with one or two potted succulent plants of the appropriate type.

Heating and Lighting Daytime air temperature to 30°C with basking areas to 40°C. Cooler at nights. Infra-red lamps or local cable heating. Broad spectrum lighting; low humidity.

Feeding Various small invertebrates and is particularly fond of locust nymphs and grasshoppers. Regular vitamin/mineral supplement. Although infrequent drinkers it is wise to fill a hollow in a rock with fresh water daily.

Community Should only be kept with lizards of similar size and habit.

Hardun *Agama stellio*
Family: Agamidae
Length: 35cm (14in)

Description The hardun is a thickset agamid with strong limbs and a thick tail. The body is covered with transverse rows of spiny scales arranged almost in a pattern of girdles. It is brownish-grey in colour with lighter markings on the body and tail.

Range South-west Europe, Asia Minor and northern Saudi Arabia.
Habitat and Habits Found in sandy and rocky areas, stone walls, and ruins.
Housing Low, semi-arid terrarium with sand and gravel substrate. A pile of stones and a climbing branch plus one or two appropriate succulent plants in concealed pots for decoration.
Heating and Lighting Up to 40°C in basking area with air temperature of about 30°C, turned off at night. Heat lamps or local cable heating. Broad spectrum lighting; low humidity.
Feeding A variety of invertebrates and baby mice. Regular vitamin/mineral supplement.
Community May be kept with lizards of similar size and habit – males are territorial. There are many other species in the genus, all of which require similar treatment.

Bearded Dragon *Amphibolurus barbatus*
Family: Agamidae
Length: 45cm (18in)

Description Named after the large inflatable throat pouch or 'beard', this species has a broad head and robust body with strong limbs. When alarmed it opens its mouth, exposing the lemon yellow interior and inflates its throat pouch. Basically dull grey in colour, darker

The bearded dragon, *Amphibolurus barbatus*, is a common Australian agamid

on the underside, it becomes suffused with yellow and white blotches when basking, or when excited.

Range Eastern and south-eastern Australia. There are about 25 other species in the genus ranging over most of the Australian continent.

Habitat and Habits A wide range of habitat from coastal wet woodland, to inland semi-desert. Diurnal and semi-arboreal, it is often seen sitting on roadside fence posts, or on recently felled tree trunks.

Housing A roomy, dry terrarium with a gravel substrate. One or two boulders, a climbing branch and a sturdy potted plant.

Heating and Lighting Infra-red lamp and local cable heater. Air temperature 25–30°C with local basking temperature up to 40°C. Cooler at night. Broad spectrum lighting; low humidity.

Feeding Various invertebrates, baby mice, regular vitamin/mineral supplement and may take some ripe fruit. Shallow water dish.

Community Should be kept only with lizards of similar size and habit.

Colour Plate No: 5.

Garden Tree Lizard *Calotes versicolor*
Family: Agamidae
Length: 35cm (14in)

Description The body is laterally compressed and the head triangular. A spiny crest extends from the nape of the neck, along the back, and into the base of the long, slender tail. The basic colour is yellowish-brown, but when excited the males take on a number of additional hues, including a red head.

Range India, Ceylon and southern China. There are several other species in the genus from the south and south-eastern Asiatic region.

Habitat and Habits Diurnal and arboreal, often seen in the neighbourhood of human habitations, including gardens, parks, and adjoining scrubland. Very agile in its leafy environment.

Housing A large, tall, planted terrarium with adequate climbing facilities. Good ventilation is essential. Greenhouse accommodation is ideal.

Heating and Lighting Basking temperatures to 35°C, air temperature 25–28°C, lowered to 22–24°C at night. Infra-red lamp; aquarium heater in water container. Broad spectrum lighting; medium to high humidity (vary with season).

Feeding Small invertebrates and regular vitamin/mineral supplement. Water dish or small pond, together with regular spraying of plant foliage.

Community Should not be kept with smaller lizards, which it will devour.

Bell's Agama *Leiolepis belliana*
Family: Agamidae
Length: 45cm (18in)

Description This species has a flat body and a smallish head; there is no spinal crest and the limbs are sturdy. The colour of the dorsal surface is olive-brown, sprinkled with dark bordered spots of a lighter colour. A number of alternating blue and orange vertical bands extend along the flanks. When the male is excited the neck and limbs take on a reddish colour. The belly is yellowish-orange.
Range South-east Asia.
Habitat and Habits A diurnal ground dwelling species which lives in burrows, coming out to forage during the day. When disturbed it retreats to its burrow with great speed.
Housing A large, low terrarium with deep, coarse sand substrate. Decorative stones and bleached tree root. An artificial, controllable hiding tunnel can be added.
Heating and Lighting Air temperature to 25°C with local basking areas to 30°C. Cooler at night. Infra-red and cable heaters. Broad spectrum lighting; low to medium humidity (seasonal).
Feeding Various invertebrates, vitamin/mineral supplement, and may take some green food. A small container of water.
Community May be kept with lizards of similar size.

Water Dragon *Physignathus cocincinus*
Family: Agamidae
Length: 80cm (31½in)

Description At first sight, this species resembles *Iguana iguana* as it is similar in shape, though smaller. Its body is bright green with tinges of blue around the throat; the long, whiplike tail is banded with brown.
Range Indo-China, south-east Asia.
Habitat and Habits Like *I. iguana*, this diurnal species lives in thickly wooded areas close to water, where it quickly takes refuge if danger approaches. It is an excellent swimmer.
Housing A large aqua-terrarium with land and water areas roughly the same size. Sturdy climbing branches which reach over the water. Robust plants should be used.
Heating and Lighting Air temperature to 28°C and water temperature of 25°C. Aquarium heaters and infra-red lamp; broad spectrum lighting; high humidity.
Feeding Larger invertebrates, small mice, dog and cat food, lean meat, and may take some soft fruit. Regular vitamin/mineral sup-

Water dragon, *Physignathus cocincinus*. Another semi-aquatic species from south-east Asia requiring humid conditions

plement. Plenty of water should always be available for drinking and swimming.

Community Best kept in single pairs. The closely related Leseur's water dragon, *Physignathus leseurii*, from eastern Australia and New Guinea, requires similar husbandry.

Colour Plate No: 6.

Spiny-tailed Agama *Uromastyx acanthinurus*
Family: Agamidae
Length: 35cm (14in)

Description This is a bizarre species much in demand by the terrarium keeper. The thickset body is dorsoventrally flattened and the head is large and triangular. The most noticeable feature is the thick, spiny tail. During rest periods the basic colour is a dull olive-brown to blackish, but as it warms itself up during basking it takes on a marbling of bright yellow and black on the body – the head almost jet black.

Range North Africa.

Habitat and Habits A semi-desert inhabitant that may live in burrows or rocky crevices. Strictly diurnal and terrestrial.

Housing A low, desert type terrarium with a deep sandy substrate and several rocks. Controllable hiding tunnels can be constructed. Planting is pointless as the lizards will eat them.

Heating and Lighting Air temperature 25–30°C with basking areas up to 40°C. Heat lamp or heat-pad (rather than cable). Broad spectrum lighting; low humidity.

Feeding This species is largely herbivorous and newly captured specimens are difficult to wean onto normal fruit and vegetables. Yellow flowers, however, particularly dandelions, are almost guaranteed to attract them. Eventually, they will take a wide range of fruit and vegetables. Some will take mealworms and locusts. A small dish of water should be available.

Community Will live in community, even with smaller species.

FAMILY: Chamaeleons—Chamaeleonidae

The chamaeleons are perhaps the most amazing group of lizards, with their highly ridged, laterally compressed bodies, granular skin capable of remarkable colour change, and opposed digits of the feet – permanently fused in groups of two and three. Other unique adaptations include the sticky, club-shaped tongue, which can be accurately projected at insect prey some distance away, and the eyes which move independently of each other. The eyelids are fused together to encircle the eye with a cone shaped mound, with a small

Striped chamaeleon, *Chamaeleo bitaeniatus*. An unusual photograph showing a captive pair mating (*Neier, Reptilianzoo Neier, Austria*)

aperture at the centre. External ear openings are not evident and the long tail is prehensile. The teeth are acrodont.

There are 2 genera and about 50 species of these highly specialised lizards; all are arboreal and insectivorous, moving slowly and methodically along the branches in search of prey which they can spot at some distance. They then stalk slowly forward until in shooting distance of the tongue, which is shot rapidly out, the prey adhering to the sticky end which is drawn back into the mouth. Chamaeleons range from southern Europe through to India, the whole of Africa and, in particular, Madagascar. There are both egglayers and livebearers in the family. Formerly, chamaeleons were regarded as notoriously difficult captives, but the secret seems to be the provision of roomy and airy quarters with plenty of natural sunlight and a varied invertebrate diet. During suitable weather they may be placed in a tree, or shrub, in the garden, where they will benefit from the fresh air and sunshine.

Striped Chamaeleon *Chamaeleo bitaeniatus*
Family: Chamaeleonidae
Length: 20cm (8in)

Description This is one of the smaller chamaeleon species and does relatively well in captivity. Like several other species, it has a helmetlike head adornment, and a sawlike crest along the back. The normal colour is olive green with yellowish highlights along the flanks. There is a narrow black stripe on either side of the head. They are livebearers.
Range East Africa.
Habitat and Habits Diurnal, it inhabits the mountain forests, which have a cool night climate.
Housing A tall terrarium with adequate climbing branches and a few robust plants. Good ventilation is important but without cold draughts.
Heating and Lighting Air temperature around 25°C during the day, lowered to 16°C at night. Infra-red heater; aquarium heater in the water and unfiltered, natural sunlight when possible. Broad spectrum lighting with ultra-violet is essential.
Feeding Requires a great variety of small invertebrate food, soon tiring of a monotonous diet. Adequate use of the sweep net should be made. Regular vitamin/mineral supplement should be given. Drinks water droplets from the foliage which must be sprayed daily.
Community Best kept in single pairs. Males are territorial; although they may not injure each other, stress in a small area may put them off their food.

Jackson's Chamaeleon *Chamaeleo jacksoni*
Family: Chamaeleonidae
Length: 30cm (12in)

Description Probably the most frequently obtainable species – and certainly very popular – the Jackson's, or three-horned, chamaeleon is remarkable in that the male possesses three 'horns': the middle one, on the tip of the snout, curves gently upwards whilst those over each eye point forward. The female has only vestigeal signs of these appendages. The colour may be bright green, through olive, to grey and brown, often with whitish flecks and blotches.
Range West Africa.
Habitat and Habits A diurnal arboreal species found in forests up to an altitude of 914m (3,000ft) above sea level.
Housing As for *C. bitaeniatus*, though somewhat larger.
Heating and Lighting As for *C. bitaeniatus*.
Feeding As for *C. bitaeniatus*.
Community More tolerant than other *Chamaeleo* species.
Colour Plate Nos: 7 and 8.

FAMILY: Skinks—Scincidae

The skinks form a large lacertilian family comprising 50 genera and over 600 species. They share with the geckos the distinction of being the only group with species on six continents. Most skinks are elongate in appearance and the trunk is more or less circular in cross section. There is usually little evidence of a neck, the small, pointed head running directly into the body. In most species the scales are smooth, glossy, and overlapping. The legs are usually short, but in some species much reduced, or absent altogether; tail length varies from very short to very long; the tongue is short and usually notched; teeth are pleurodont.
Cosmopolitan in the warmer parts of the world, the skinks are terrestrial or burrowing species. Most are insectivorous but some are partly herbivorous. Many species are colourful and take well to captivity, some breeding fairly readily. There are both oviparous and ovo-viviparous forms.

Snake-eyed Skink *Ablepharus kitaibeli*
Family: Scincidae
Length: 12cm (5in)

Description This slim, long-bodied skink has very short limbs and a relatively thick tail. The head is small and the snout pointed. The skin is extremely glossy. As its common name implies, this species lacks movable eyelids, the transparent spectacle being changed with the slough, just as in snakes. Their colour is olive or bronze brown above, darker on the flanks and sometimes has rows of dark and light spots.

Range Eastern Europe, Asia Minor, northern Saudi Arabia.

Habitat and Habits Found mainly in low-lying areas, in meadows, sunny slopes and banks, and scrubland. Moves under leaf litter and vegetation, occasionally coming out to bask. Diurnal but active on warm nights.

Housing Low, woodland type terrarium with sand, peat and loam substrate. A few flat stones as hiding places and a couple of grass clumps for decoration.

Heating and Lighting Air temperature around 25°C during the day, cooler at night. Basking area to 30°C. Small heat lamp; broad spectrum lighting; medium humidity.

Feeding Small invertebrates, will take earthworms and bloodworms. Regular vitamin/mineral supplement and small water container.

Hibernation A period of 8 to 10 weeks at reduced temperature is recommended.

Community Only with lizards of similar size.

Eyed Skink *Chalcides ocellatus*
Family: Scincidae
Length: 20cm (8in)

Description This species has a typical skinklike, robust body, short limbs and a shortish tail. As its name suggests, it has a sprinkling of black bordered, white 'eye' spots on the upper side of its bronze coloured body. The underside is white.

Range South-eastern Europe, Mediterranean islands, North Africa, western Asia.

Habitat and Habits Prefers sandy scrub areas, vineyards, stone walls, and ruins. Mainly diurnal, but active at night in warm weather. Keeps to the ground, hiding under stones or in burrows.

Housing Low, semi-desert terrarium with a mixture of coarse sand and gravel substrate. Flat stones for hiding and basking; one or two low, potted, succulent plants; piece of olive wood or vine stem as decoration.

Heating and Lighting Daytime air temperature to 30°C; basking area up to 38°C. Infra-red lamp or heat cable (local). Cooler at night. Broad spectrum lighting; low humidity.

Feeding Various small invertebrates and regular vitamin/mineral supplement. Shallow water container.

Hibernation Those from the northern part of the range require a 4–6 week rest period at reduced temperature.

Colour Plate No: 9.

Cunningham's Skink *Egernia cunninghami*
Family: Scincidae
Length: 40cm (16in)

Description A feature of the skinks in the genus *Egernia* is the keeled, pointed scales which give them a slightly spiny appearance, particularly noticeable in the tail. The body is typically skinklike and the head relatively large. The limbs are strongly built. The body colour of the male ranges from buff to dark brown; the female shows a pinkish tinge. A sprinkling of light coloured spots covers the darker areas and the underside is reddish-brown to dark brown.

Range South-western Australia.

Habitat and Habits A rock dwelling species that hides in crevices, or under large slabs of stone. Diurnal.

Housing A large, low terrarium furnished with rocky shelves and ledges, with controllable hiding places. Gravel substrate and one or two robust potted plants situated such that the lizards cannot damage them.

Feeding An omnivorous species taking fruit and vegetables, as well as the usual invertebrates. Fond of rice pudding and jam! Regular vitamin/mineral supplement. Shallow water container.

Community May be kept in groups.

Five-lined Skink *Eumeces fasciatus*
Family: Scincidae
Length: 23cm (9in)

Description A fairly slender lizard with a long, elegant tail and a smallish head. The five-lined skink is remarkable in that the young are so different in colour from the adults, that at one time it was thought they were different species. The hatchlings are black, with white or yellow stripes running into a bright blue tail. As the skink grows, the bright colours are gradually lost until a fairly plain brown adult results. The males have a reddish tinge on the head.

Range Eastern USA.

Habitat and Habits A terrestrial and diurnal lizard inhabiting open woodland.

Housing A low type, woodland terrarium. Substrate is a mixture of sand, loam and leaf litter; one or two prostrate potted plants and a grass clump.

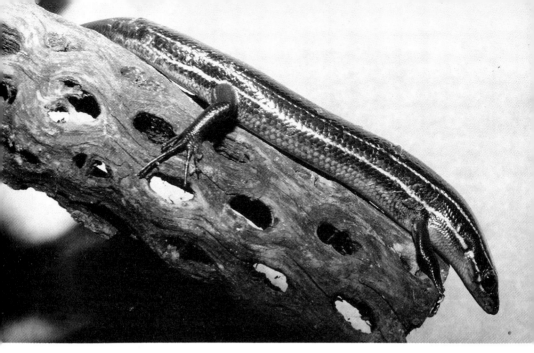

This glossy fellow is the five-lined skink, *Eumeces inexpectatus* from North America

Heating and Lighting Air temperature around 25°C; local basking temperature to 32°C. Aquarium heater in water container; small heat lamp; semi-humid.

Feeding A variety of small invertebrates.

Hibernation A rest period of 10–12 weeks at 10–15°C is recommended.

Community Not to be kept with smaller lizards. A closely related species, the red-headed skink, *Eumeces laticeps*, requires similar husbandry.

Berber Skink *Eumeces schneiderii*
Family: Scincidae
Length: 40cm (16in)

Description The Berber skink is a popular terrarium inmate. Similar in shape to *Chalcides ocellatus*, but larger and more robust, this species is attractively coloured. The dorsal surface is rust brown with a series of black bands and orange spots traversing the body. The underside is whitish.

Range North Africa.

Habitat and Habits In scrub areas, usually near to water, and often found in gardens and plantations. They make long, shallow burrows as retreats. Diurnal.

Housing A large, low, semi-desert terrarium with substrate of coarse sand and gravel to 10cm (4in) depth. Plants should be anchored with large pebbles.

Heating and Lighting Air temperature 27–30°C, local basking temperature to 35°C. Cooler at night. Infra-red lamp or local cable heating. Broad spectrum lighting; low humidity.

Feeding Small invertebrates, lean meat, dog and cat food and some soft fruit. Regular vitamin/mineral supplement. Shallow water container.

Community Best kept in pairs.

African Five-lined Skink *Mabuya quinquetaeniata*
Family: Scincidae
Length: 25cm (10in)

Description Typically skinklike in shape. The males are very colourful with a bronze body, broken with black and white spots, and exhibiting a multi-coloured iridescent sheen. The elegant tail is orange, whilst that of the young is bright blue – which is retained by the otherwise relatively dull coloured female.

Range Southern Africa.

Habitat and Habits Scrubland and cultivated areas where it is extremely active during the day. Hides under dense, low-lying vegetation or in burrows.

Housing Low, scrubland type terrarium with one or two rocks and climbing branches, and a potted plant. Substrate of sand and peat mixture.

African Five-lined skink, *Mabuya quinquetaeniata*. A very colourful species from Southern Africa

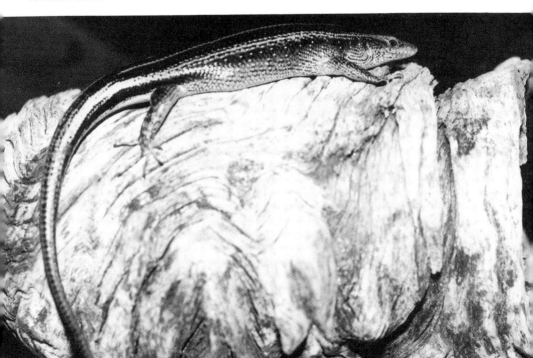

Heating and Lighting Daytime air temperature to 28°C; cooler at night. Local cable heating or heat lamp; medium humidity (seasonal).
Feeding Small invertebrates and regular vitamin/mineral supplement. Water container.
Community Satisfactory with lizards of similar size and habit.

Striped Skink *Mabuya striata*
Family: Scincidae
Length: 20cm (8in)

Description Although not particularly colourful, the little striped skink is a hardy and interesting terrarium inmate. The body is a plain bronze brown, broken by a yellowish stripe down each side of the back. Underside is yellowish.
Range Eastern and southern Africa.
Habitat and Habits Diurnal, it is found at medium altitudes, usually not far from water, and common in gardens and plantations – even on the walls of dwellings.
Housing As for *M. quinquetaeniata*.
Heating and Lighting As for *M. quinquetaeniata*.
Feeding As for *M. quinquetaeniata*.
Community Good with lizards of similar size and habit. Males are territorial.

Blue-tongued Skink *Tiliqua scincoides*
Family: Scincidae
Length: 45cm (18in)

Description The blue-tongued skink was one of the best loved terrarium inmates, but export bans from Australia make it impossible to obtain, other than captive bred specimens. Typically skinklike in shape, but robust and with a shortish tail, it is silvery grey to light brown in colour with a series of darker cross bands; underside is whitish. The tongue is bright blue.
Range Northern and eastern Australia.
Habitat and Habits A diurnal, terrestrial species found in a range of habitats from open woodland to dry grassland. Retreats under leaf litter or logs at night. Livebearer, producing up to 25 young.
Housing A large, low terrarium with fine-grade shingle as substrate; some leaf litter on its surface and an arrangement of rocks in the background. Due to the burrowing activities of these lizards, planting is pointless.
Heating and Lighting Air temperature to 30°C with local basking temperature to 35°C. Infra-red lamp or local cable or pad heating; broad spectrum lighting.

Feeding Large insects, snails, fruit and vegetables, dog and cat food, and regular vitamin/mineral supplement. Large water bath as the animals like to bathe.
Community Best kept in single pairs. May become very tame.
Colour Plate No: 10.

Shingleback *Trachydosaurus rugosus*
Family: Scincidae
Length: 35cm (14in)

Description The body is typically skinklike in shape but the tail is short and stumpy. The scales are thick and overlapping, almost resembling a pine cone. Usually dark brown above, with yellowish blotches – especially on the sides. Underside is whitish.
Range Southern and eastern Australia.
Habitat and Habits Found mainly in dry scrubland. Diurnal, sheltering under vegetation and fallen timber at night. A slow moving terrestrial lizard.
Housing A large, desert type terrarium. Substrate of coarse sand and shingle with a dead tree stump and a few rocks as decoration. Planting is pointless.
Heating and Lighting As for *Tiliqua scincoides*.
Feeding Lean meat, dog and cat food, large insects, snails, soft fruit and regular vitamin/mineral supplement. Shallow water container.
Community Good with lizards of similar size and may become tame.

FAMILY: Girdled and Plated Lizards—Cordylidae

The family contains some 40 species in 10 genera divided into 2 subfamilies, the Cordylinae (girdled lizards) and the Gerrhosaurinae (plated lizards). The former are typically spiny with girdles of enlarged scales around the body and especially around the tail, which is used as a 'club' to deter predators. Some species are flattened as an adaptation for living in rock crevices. The Gerrhosaurinae have osteoderms (bony plates) beneath their scales which create an effective body armour. In most species the limbs are well developed. The teeth are pleurodont and all species feed on small animals. They are distributed widely over Africa, south of the Sahara, and on the island of Madagascar. Many of these species do well in captivity and breeding occurs sporadically, though by no means regularly enough. The girdled lizards (often called zonures) are ovo-viviparous, usually bearing a small number of live young; the plated lizards lay eggs (oviparous).

Giant Zonure, Sungazer *Cordylus giganteus*
Subfamily: Cordylinae
Length: 35cm (14in)

Description The largest of the girdled lizards. Known as the sungazer on account of its habit of holding its head up when basking. It is a sturdily built lizard with spiny scales all over the back and tail, which is whipped about as a defensive measure (it has been known to draw blood on the human hand) but is not a dangerous lizard. The scales are mainly dark brown with a scattering of dark blotches. The belly scales are broad and speckled black over greyish-white.
Range Southern Africa.
Habitat and Habits Lives in the area of rocky outcrops where it has a good vantage point, and basks in the sun for long periods.
Housing A large airy terrarium with gravel substrate. Artificial rock formations with ample basking ledges. One or two succulent plants.
Heating and Lighting Air temperature 30°C, with local basking temperatures to 45°C. Heating cable (local) or infra-red lamps. Broad spectrum lighting; low humidity.
Feeding Large invertebrates (particularly fond of cockroaches and beetles), lean meat, dog and cat food, raw eggs, chopped mice, and day old chicks. Regular vitamin/mineral supplement. Small water container.
Community Good with lizards of similar size and habit. Several other species of girdled lizard, such as *C. cataphractus*, *C. cordylus*, *C. jonesi*, and *C. warreni*, require similar husbandry.
Colour Plate No: 11.

Sudan Plated Lizard *Gerrhosaurus major*
Subfamily: Gerrhosaurinae
Length: 40cm (16in)

Description A robust lizard with its squarish scales arranged in rings both around the body, and its long, tapered tail. The body is dark brown on the back, and yellow on the underside.
Range Sudan.
Habitat and Habits Found in dry, sparsely vegetated areas amongst rocks and scree. A diurnal, sun loving species.
Housing A large, semi-desert type terrarium with rock formation and adequate basking ledges; one or two potted plants sunk into the gravel substrate.
Heating and Lighting Daytime air temperature to 28°C with local basking temperature to 35°C. Infra-red lamp or local cable or pad heating. Broad spectrum lighting; low humidity.

(top) Sudan plated lizard, *Gerrhosaurus major*. A robust but docile species, suited to the warm, dry terrarium. (above) The yellow-throated plated lizard, *Gerrhosaurus validus* is a docile and friendly species which soon settles into captivity

Feeding Large invertebrates, baby mice, dog and cat food, lean meat and regular vitamin/mineral supplement; may take some soft fruit. Shallow water container.

Community Good with lizards of similar size and habit. Several other species of plated lizard, including *G. flavigularis*, *G. nigrolineatus*, and *G. validus*, require similar husbandry.

Ornamental Flat Lizard *Platysaurus guttatus*
Subfamily: Cordylinae
Length: 24cm (10in)

Description Although in the same subfamily as the girdled lizards there appear to be only a few obvious similarities. *Platysaurus* has a smooth skin with small, granular scales and it is only in the long, tapered tail that the subdued spiny girdles occur. The remarkable thing about *Platysaurus* is its extreme dorsolaterally flattened form, an adaptation for squeezing into narrow rock crevices. Basic colour is brown but suffused with green and blue, especially under warm conditions. A series of stripes run along the back, interspersed with light blotches; the tail is orange.

Range Southern Africa.

Habitat and Habits Rocky outcrops with plenty of narrow cracks and crevices. A highly active, sunloving lizard.

Housing A roomy terrarium furnished with artificial rock faces containing controllable crevices as hiding places. Coarse sand and gravel substrate. A climbing branch and one or two potted plants for decoration.

Heating and Lighting Daytime air temperature around 28°C with local basking temperature to 35°C. Cable heater (local) or infra-red lamp. Broad spectrum lighting; low humidity.

Feeding Small invertebrates and regular vitamin/mineral supplement. Water may be given in a rocky hollow.

Community Good with lizards of similar size and habit. Other species, including *P. intermedius* and *P. capensis*, require similar husbandry.

FAMILY: Typical Lizards—Lacertidae

This family contains the old world 'typical' lizards. All are similar in general shape, with elongate body, well developed limbs, and a long, slender tail – which can be shed at times of danger (autotomy). The head is usually well defined from the body by a narrower neck. The scales are mainly granular, those on the head enlarged and fused to the skull. The teeth are pleurodont and the tongue is long, extensible and deeply forked. Most are insectivorous but some of the larger species will take small vertebrates.

There are some 70 species in about 20 genera, distributed throughout Africa, Europe and Asia. In captivity, many of the species thrive and breed frequently, provided the correct conditions are given. Many of the European species are ideal for outdoor reptiliaries. Most are egglayers but some bear live young.

Spiny-footed Lizard *Acanthodactylus erythrurus*
Subfamily: Lacertidae
Length: 19cm (7in)

Description Typically lacertid in form but quite robust, this lizard has fringes of spiny scales on its toes, which enable it to move speedily over loose sand. The colour is very variable but usually light brown on the back and darker on the sides. The body sports a series of six narrow, longitudinal white stripes interspersed with dark blotches and yellow spots. The underside is pale yellow. Juveniles are striped black and white with an orange tail.

Range Iberian peninsula and North Africa.

Habitat and Habits A terrestrial and diurnal sun loving lizard, usually found in sparsely vegetated sandy areas. May be found on coastal sand dunes. When disturbed it hides in dense vegetation or in shallow burrows.

Housing Low, dry terrarium with medium gauge sandy substrate. A few pebbles and grass clumps for decoration and shelter.

Heating and Lighting Daytime air temperature around 28°C with local basking temperature to 35°C. Natural sunlight when possible. Infra-red lamp or cable heating (local). Broad spectrum lighting; dry to medium humidity.

Feeding Variety of small invertebrates and regular vitamin/mineral supplement. Small dish of water.

Hibernation A period of 4–6 weeks at reduced temperature is recommended.

Community Good with lizards of similar size and habit. Several other North African and Saudi Arabian species require similar husbandry.

Colour Plate No: 12 – a related genus.

Dwarf Keeled Lizard *Algyroides fitzingeri*
Family: Lacertidae
Length: 12cm (5in)

Description This very small lacertid has a body covering of keeled, pointed scales, giving it a vaguely spiny appearance. The dorsal surface is a uniform nut brown, merging into pale grey on the throat; the underside is yellowish.

Range Corsica and Sardinia.

Habitat and Habits Found in scrub and rocky slopes. Sometimes on stone walls or on tree trunks. Diurnal, but prefers semi-shade.

Housing Small, low terrarium; sandy substrate with piles of stones. Low succulent plants in pots, sunk into substrate, or hidden behind rocks.

Heating and Lighting Air temperature 28–30°C with local basking temperature to 35°C. Infra-red lamp or cable heater (local). Broad spectrum lighting.

Feeding Very small invertebrates and regular vitamin/mineral supplement.

Hibernation Short rest period recommended.

Community Good with lizards of similar size and habit.

Eyed lizard, *Lacerta lepida*. Europe's largest lizard

Eyed Lizard *Lacerta lepida*
Family: Lacertidae
Length: 60cm (23½in)

Description The largest European lacertid, powerfully built and with strong jaws capable of giving a painful bite. The ground colour of the body is rich green, covered with a sprinkling of yellow and dark green dots. The most outstanding feature is the rows of bright blue spots along the flanks. The underside is usually greeny-yellow.

Range Iberian peninsula, southern France, north-west Italy, and North-west Africa.

Habitat and Habits Prefers open woodland and scrub up to an altitude of 2,000m (6,500ft). Sometimes seen in olive groves or vineyards. Hides in dense vegetation, hollow trees, or piles of stones.

Housing Very large terrarium or, preferably, greenhouse accommodation. May be kept in outside reptiliary in summer months, or even all year round if suitable hibernating chambers are provided.

Heating and Lighting Natural sunlight, infra-red lamps or cable heaters. Prefers air temperature at 30°C, cooler at night. Adequate heated basking areas should be provided. Broad spectrum lighting; low to medium humidity.

Feeding Large invertebrates, young mice, raw eggs, condensed milk, lean meat, dog and cat food, soft fruit and regular vitamin/mineral supplement.

Hibernation Winter rest period of 6–8 weeks recommended.

Community Best kept in single pairs.

Green Lizard *Lacerta viridis*
Family: Lacertidae
Length: 40cm (16in)

Description An elegant lizard with a tail twice as long as the body. The colour of the dorsal surface is grass green, sprinkled liberally with yellow and dark green dots. In the breeding season the male's throat becomes sky blue. The female and juveniles are a somewhat duller, olive green, sometimes with a series of lighter and darker stripes along the back.
Range Central and southern Europe.
Habitat and Habits Diurnal in open woodland, heathland, hedgerows, plantations and other densely vegetated places. Climbs into shrubs in search of prey. Takes refuge in dense vegetation when pursued.
Housing Large, airy terrarium, greenhouse accommodation or outdoor reptiliaries with ample climbing and basking areas. Substrate of medium grade gravel.
Heating and Lighting Air temperature around 25°C with basking areas hotter. Natural sunlight, heat lamps or cable heating. Broad spectrum lighting; low to medium humidity.
Feeding Large invertebrates, baby mice, lean meat, dog and cat food, soft fruit and regular vitamin/mineral supplement. Large water dish.
Hibernation Winter rest period for 8–10 weeks at lower temperature advised.
Community Territorial, best kept in pairs.
Colour Plate No: 13.

Viviparous Lizard *Lacerta vivipara*
Family: Lacertidae
Length: 18cm (7in)

Description The common lizard of Europe. Delicate in build but typically lacertid in shape. Colours are very variable but usually consist of stripes and blotches in various shades of brown. The underside is orange to red in the males, whitish in the females.
Range Across central and northern Europe, through Asia to the Pacific Ocean.
Habitat and Habits A wide range of habitat from coastal heathland to open woodland, hedgerow to mountain slope. Found inside the Arctic Circle. Ovo-viviparous producing 6–12 live young in the summer. Diurnal.
Housing Unheated woodland type terrarium, or outdoor reptiliary. In absence of adequate sunshine, an infra-red lamp and broad spectrum lighting can be used. Air temperature to 25°C during the day, reduce to 16°C at night. Medium humidity.

Feeding Wide variety of small invertebrates, especially spiders, and regular vitamin/mineral supplement. Water dish.
Hibernation A full hibernation period of not less than 3 months is recommended.
Community May be kept with lizards of similar size and habit.

Wall Lizard *Podarcis* (formerly *Lacerta*) *muralis*
Family: Lacertidae
Length: 18cm (7in)

Description The wall lizard comes in so many variations of colour that it is difficult to describe. May be various shades of brown, green or black, with or without stripes of varying colours. The female is usually less spectacularly patterned.
Range Central and southern Europe (at least 20 subspecies).
Habitat and Habits Diurnal, it is found on sunny rocky slopes, stone walls, ruins, vineyards and hedgerows.
Housing Large, airy terrarium with sand and gravel substrate, rocks, climbing branch and a few potted plants. Also greenhouse and reptiliary accommodation.
Heating and Lighting Natural sunlight, infra-red lamp or heat cable. Daytime air temperature to 28°C with basking areas to 35°C. Broad spectrum lighting; low to medium humidity.
Feeding Various small invertebrates and regular vitamin/mineral supplement; water dish.
Hibernation A period of 8–10 weeks at a lower temperature is recommended.
Community May be kept with lizards of similar size and habit.
Colour Plate No: 13.

Ruin Lizard *Podarcis sicula*
Family: Lacertidae
Length: 25cm (10in)

Description Like *P. muralis*, there are a number of subspecies throughout its range and a great variety of colours and patterns, mostly varying shades of brown or green, even black. May be striped, reticulated or marbled.
Range Italy, Yugoslavia and Tyrrhenian islands. Introduced to many other areas.
Habitat and Habits Very common in its range, often close to human habitations. Diurnal, it is found on walls, rocky areas, scrubland, rubbish dumps and dry river beds.
Housing Large, airy terrarium or greenhouse accommodation. Sub-

Greek wall lizard, *Lacerta graeca*. Requires similar care to that described for *Podarcis sicula* (*B. Langerwerf*)

strate of coarse sand and gravel. Some rocks, a climbing branch and one or two potted plants.

Heating and Lighting As for *P. muralis*.

Feeding As for *P. muralis*.

Hibernation Short rest period.

Community May be kept with lizards of similar size and habit.

Colour Plate No: 14.

FAMILY: Tegus and Greaved Lizards—Teiidae

The teiids are a large family of lacertids forming about 40 genera and around 200 species. They are confined to the new world, but widely distributed from the northern USA through Central America to south-central Argentina and Chile. There are many forms, ranging from arboreal to desert types. Some are almost limbless burrowing species. However, the majority bear a superficial resemblance to the Euro-Asian lacertids, which they replace in the Americas. The scales are generally granular, but large and platelike on the head. The majority of species have a long tail and well developed limbs.

The tongue is extensible and forked; the teeth are subacrodont (almost on the summit of the jaws). Most species are carnivorous but some are partly or mainly herbivorous. Few species are regularly kept in captivity and those that are, often remain nervous and do not settle in well. However, with improved husbandry there is no reason why these should not now thrive. Captive breeding is sparsely documented, but most species are known to be oviparous.

The common ameiva, *Ameiva ameiva*, is an agile ground dweller from tropical South America

Ameiva *Ameiva ameiva*
Family: Teiidae
Length: 45cm (18in)

Description The ameiva bears a superficial resemblance to *Lacerta viridis*, but the head is narrower and the snout more pointed. Colour is variable, but most forms show bright green on the anterior part of the body, running into brown at the posterior part.
Range Southern Central America and northern South America.
Habitat and Habits Found in open woodland and scrub areas where it is mainly terrestrial. Diurnal, it excavates burrows into which it retires at night.
Housing A large, tropical rain forest type terrarium with sand, peat and leaf litter substrate, horizontal logs, a few foliage plants and basking areas.
Heating and Lighting Air temperature of around 30°C with basking area to 35°C. Heat lamp or cable heater; aquarium heater in pond, aerater for humidity. Night-time temperature of not less than 24°C.
Feeding Large invertebrates, including snails and earthworms, some soft fruit and regular vitamin/mineral supplement. Large water container.
Community Best kept in single pairs.

Six-lined Racerunner *Cnemidophorus sexlineatus*
Family: Teiidae
Length: 30cm (12in)

Description This and other members of the genus *Cnemidophorus* are slim, long-tailed lizards of great speed and agility, thus the common name. The head is pointed and, from the neck, six evenly spaced, yellow stripes run down the brownish body. The underside is lighter, with a bluish or greenish tinge in the males.

Range Eastern USA.

Habitat and Habits Frequently found in sandy areas, often at the sides of roads and tracks, open scrub, meadow land, and the edges of swamps. Terrestrial and diurnal, it disappears with great rapidity when disturbed.

Housing Terrarium with large floor area for these active lizards. A sand and peat mixture as substrate with some flat stones and large pebbles as decoration. Planting is best restricted to grass clumps which can be changed regularly.

Heating and Lighting Infra-red lamp or cable heater (local). Air temperature around 28°C with local basking temperature to 38°C. Cooler at night. Broad spectrum lighting; low to medium humidity.

Feeding Small invertebrates and regular vitamin/mineral supplement; small water container.

Hibernation A short, winter rest period is recommended.

Community Good with lizards of similar size and habit. Several other *Cnemidophorus* species require similar husbandry.

Golden Tegu *Tupinambis nigropunctatus*
Family: Teiidae
Length: 1m (3¼ft)

Description In shape, the tegu bears some resemblance to *Lacerta lepida*, but with a heavier build. There are a number of species in the genus of varying colours. The golden tegu is deep glossy black, marked with rows of golden yellow dots and blotches.

Range Tropical South America.

Habitat and Habits Ranges from tropical rain forest to fairly dry scrubland. An active powerful lizard which needs to be handled with care. It readily settles into captivity and becomes tame. Terrestrial and diurnal.

Housing An extremely large terrarium with at least 2sq m (2¼sq yd) floor area. Heavy gravel or shingle substrate with a few rocks and branches for decoration. Planting is unnecessary as the heavy lizards will soon damage them.

Heating and Lighting Infra-red lamp or pad heater (local). Air temperature 28–32°C with local basking temperature to 40°C. Cooler at night, but not less than 20°C. Broad spectrum lighting; medium to high humidity.

Feeding Will take well to a staple diet of raw, minced lean beef, mixed with raw eggs. Should be varied with mice, chicks, and the occasional

Tegu, *Tupinambis* species

grated vegetables added to the meat mixture. Regular vitamin/mineral supplement. Large water bath (for drinking and bathing). *Community* Best kept in single pairs.

FAMILY: Limbless Skinks—Feylinidae

This is a small family of little known lizards with a single genus, *Feylinia*, and only 4 species. They are burrowing lizards living in loose soil and leaf litter. Their principal diet appears to be termites. The body is scaly, limbless and wormlike. Found in central Africa, little is known of the captive husbandry of these lizards.

FAMILY: Alligator Lizards – Slow Worms – Glass Snakes—Anguidae

This family contains about 8 genera and around 60 species distributed through North and South America, Europe and Asia. All are elongate in body form and covered with overlapping scales supported by osteoderms. In many species the limbs are reduced, or lost altogether. The tail is long and capable of being shed. The teeth are pleurodont and the tongue notched, or slightly forked. Most species feed on invertebrates, some on small vertebrates.

Slow Worm or Blind Worm *Anguis fragilis*
Subfamily: Anguinae
Length: 35cm (14in)

Description Anguis fragilis is neither blind, nor particularly slow, nor even is it a worm as its common names suggest. This limbless lizard is slimly built, with tight overlapping glossy scales. Eyelids and ear openings are plainly visible. Adults are dull bronze in colour; juveniles are copper coloured with a dark vertebral stripe. The underside is steel grey.

Range Central Europe.

Habitat and Habits A partially burrowing reptile often found under flat stones, pieces of corrugated iron, or other material lying flat on the ground. May be found in hedgerows, heathland, open woodland, and gardens. Mainly crepuscular in habit, but will bask in the early morning sun.

Housing A low, woodland type terrarium with a substrate of sand and peat, one or two flat stones, and clumps of grass.

Heating and Lighting Supplementary heating is not strictly necessary but it will appreciate summer daytime temperatures to 28°C. Broad spectrum lighting, or natural sunlight for plants.

Feeding Small invertebrates – particularly fond of small, grey slugs. Regular vitamin/mineral supplement. Small, shallow water container.

Hibernation A hibernation period of 10–12 weeks is recommended.

Community Good in community with small lizards such as *Lacerta vivipara*.

Colour Plate No: 15.

Glass Snake, Scheltopusik *Ophisaurus apodus*
Subfamily: Anguinae
Length: 1.1m (3½ft)

Description Superficially, a larger version of *Anguis fragilis*. The scales are arranged in rings around the body. It has a lateral fold of skin along the flanks, with vestigeal hind limbs at the posterior end. Basic colour is a deep bronze brown – underside is yellowish. Juveniles are ash grey with dark brown flecks and bands. The common name of glass snake refers to its long, fragile tail which is shed when under predatory attack, or if roughly handled. The regenerated tail is never as elegant as the original.

Range Eastern Europe from the Balkans into Asia Minor, and western Asia.

Habitat and Habits Found in scrub and rocky areas. May burrow or hide under stones, in stone walls, or in rotten timber. Oviparous, the female may coil around incubating eggs. Diurnal and terrestrial.

Housing A large, low terrarium with substrate of coarse sand and a portion of leaf litter, a hollow log and flat stones. Plants must be protected around the roots with heavy pebbles.
Heating and Lighting Air and floor temperature around 28°C. Heat lamp or pad heater, turned off at night. Broad spectrum lighting; low humidity.
Feeding Large invertebrates, snails, baby mice, eggs and minced, lean meat. Regular vitamin/mineral supplement and shallow water container.
Hibernation Winter rest period of 4–6 weeks at reduced temperature.
Community Good with lizards of similar size, but will devour smaller ones.
Colour Plate No: 16.

Southern Alligator Lizard *Gerrhonotus multicarinatus*
Subfamily: Gerrhonotinae
Length: 30cm (12in)

Description An elongate lizard with short but well developed limbs and a long semi-prehensile tail. A lateral skin fold between fore and rear limbs is present. Colour is a mixture of browns, black and yellow, arranged in bars and blotches.
Range South-western USA.
Habitat and Habits Semi-arboreal and diurnal it is commonly found in low shrubs and plants.
Housing A large, tall terrarium with substrate of sand, peat and leaf litter. Climbing branches and creeping plants together with a pile of rocks as hiding places.
Heating and Lighting Air temperature around 25°C with local basking temperature to 35°C. Heat lamp and aquarium heater in water container. Medium humidity.
Feeding Small invertebrates and regular vitamin/mineral supplement. Shallow water dish; spray plants with water 2–3 times per week.
Hibernation Short, winter rest period at reduced temperature.
Community Best kept with their own species.
Colour Plate No: 17.

FAMILY: Burrowing Slow Worms—Anniellidae

A family containing only 1 genus and 2 species confined to central and coastal California in the USA. The small, limbless body is covered with scales and there are no apparent external ear openings. The eyes are small. The teeth are pleurodont and the tongue forked. They feed on small invertebrates and are ovo-viviparous. Literature on the husbandry of these species is sparse.

24 Corn snake, *Elaphe guttata*; a colourful, docile and popular snake

25 One of the many subspecies of the kingsnake, *Lampropeltis getulus floridana*, is from Florida

26 Milksnake, *Lampropeltis triangulum*; an attractive, brightly coloured snake which will do well in captivity

27 Mangrove snake, *Boiga dendrophila*; a mildly venomous snake, though generally considered harmless to man. Nonetheless, it should be treated with the respect its rear fangs dictate

FAMILY: Crocodile Lizard – Strange Lizards—Xenosauridae

In this family of 2 genera and 4 species, the limbs are well developed and the body covered by scales supported by osteoderms. The teeth are pleurodont. The crocodile lizard, *Shinisaurus crocodilurus*, from southern China, is a semi-aquatic species of about 35cm (14in) in length, feeding on small fish, tadpoles, and aquatic invertebrates. The strange lizard genus, *Xenosaurus*, has 3 species in central and southern Mexico; they range in size from 25 to 40cm (10–16in) and are primarily insectivorous. Little is known of the captive husbandry of these reptiles.

FAMILY: Monitor Lizards—Varanidae

The monitor lizards are all contained in the single genus *Varanus*, in which there are about 30 species. Two-thirds of these are found in Australia, the remainder scattered about the old world tropics. The world's largest lizard, the Komodo dragon, *V. komodoensis*, from the island of Komodo and some adjoining islands, is a member of this genus. Most other species are fairly large. The body is elongate with well developed limbs and a long, whiplike tail which is often laterally flattened. The head is long and the snout pointed, with powerful jaws. The teeth are pleurodont and the tongue long, retractile, and deeply forked. All are carnivorous, feeding on a wide range of invertebrates, vertebrates, eggs and carrion. Many species do well in captivity, although breeding is not often accomplished. The huge size to which many species grow makes them unsuitable for the average household, though many, especially if reared from juveniles, become extremely tame and trusting.

The perentie, *Varanus giganteus*. The largest Australian monitor. Specimens up to 2·5m (7½ft) have been recorded (*Dave Barker, Dallas*)

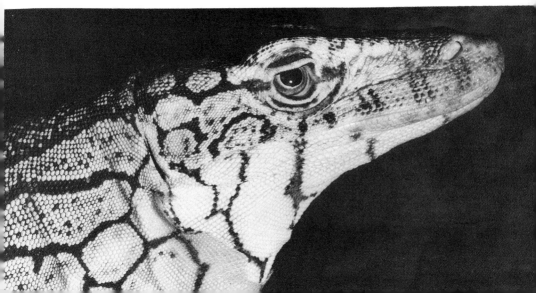

The savannah monitor, *Varanus exanthematicus*, can be quite belligerent when newly captured, but soon settles down to become docile

Savannah Monitor *Varanus exanthematicus*
Family: Varanidae
Length: 1m (3¼ft)

Description This species has a broader head and blunter snout than most other varanids. It is heavily built with granular scales covering the body. The basic colour is yellowish-grey to brown, with a number of lighter spots and blotches.

Range Savannah regions of eastern and southern Africa.

Habitat and Habits A diurnal terrestrial inhabitant of the African savannah.

Housing Monitors require large, strong accommodation, preferably brick built, and with a concrete floor with a pond incorporated. The faeces of monitors is voluminous and fluid, so adequate washing down facilities should be incorporated into the housing. Stout climbing branches and rock ledges should be provided. Planting would be pointless.

Heating and Lighting Central heating with air convection is the best method of heating monitor accommodation; alternatively, heat lamps, or electric heaters made safe behind strong wire mesh. Air and floor temperatures around 30°C. Broad spectrum lighting; low to medium humidity (seasonal).

Feeding Dead mice, rats, day old chicks, lean meat, offal, eggs and regular vitamin/mineral supplement. Fresh water in pond daily.

Community Relatively good with lizards of similar size. Other species of monitor occasionally available include the Nile monitor, *V. niloticus*, the rough-necked monitor, *V. rudicollis*, and the Asian water monitor, *V. salvator*. All require similar husbandry and accommodation compatible with their size.   *Colour Plate No:* 18 – related species.

FAMILY: Gila Monster – Beaded Lizard—Helodermatidae

These are the only venomous lizards and can be kept only under licence in the UK. There are only two species in a single genus, found in south-western USA and Mexico. The stout body with short, well developed limbs and short, thick tail is covered with small, granular scales supported by osteoderms. The head is broad and the teeth pleurodont, those in the lower jaw bearing grooves to conduct poison from a number of labial glands. In the wild they feed on small mammals, nestling birds and eggs.

Gila Monster *Heloderma suspectum* (venomous)
Family: Helodermatidae
Length: 48cm (19in)

Description The broad head, plump body and fat tail of this species is covered with beadlike scales. The basic colour is black with an irregular pattern of orange-red blotches.
Range South-western USA, Mexico.
Habitat and Habits A desert dwelling semi-noctural species which lives

The beaded lizard, *Heloderma horridum*, is one of only two species of venomous lizard, the other being the gila monster, *Heloderma suspectum*

in burrows during the day. Slow moving, but capable of a lightning bite and *definitely* not recommended for the beginner. Although fatalities are rare from the bite of this species, and the closely related *H. horridum*, they have been known to occur.Oviparous.

Housing A low, desert type terrarium with gravel substrate and an artificial controllable burrow. The access doors should be secured with padlocks at all times, except for routine cleaning.

Heating and Lighting Heat cable under gravel or infra-red lamps. Daytime air temperature to 35°C, cooler at night. Broad spectrum lighting; low humidity.

Feeding In captivity, this species seems to do well only on chopped, lean meat mixed with raw eggs. Regular vitamin/mineral supplement should be added. Large water dish in which the lizards will bathe.

Community Best kept in single pairs. The beaded lizard, *Heloderma horridum*, from western Mexico, requires similar husbandry, but larger accommodation.

FAMILY: Earless Monitor—Lanthonotidae

This family contains only a single species, the earless monitor, *Lanthonotus borneensis*, a rare and local species – first discovered in 1878. Found only in north-west Borneo, this unusual lizard lives near watercourses which it frequently enters, presumably in search of food said to consist primarily of aquatic animals. The species reaches a length of about 40cm (16in). The head is broad and flattened, the neck thick, extending into an elongate body and shortish, blunt-ended tail. There is no external ear opening and only the lower eyelid, which has a transparent window, is movable. Longitudinal rows of keeled scales run the length of the plain, dark brown body. Little is documented on the care of this reptile, but captive specimens have been known to feed on strips of raw fish.

SUBORDER: Amphisbaenia

FAMILY: Amphisbaenians—Amphisbaenidae

European Amphisbaenian *Blanus cinereus*
Family: Amphisbaenidae
Length: 20cm (8in)

Description At first sight, this species bears a remarkable resemblance to a large earthworm. The scales are arranged in concentric rings around the body to resemble segments. The eyes are vestigeal and just visible, and the ears are covered by the skin. The body is greyish to reddish-brown, the underside being somewhat lighter.

Range The Iberian peninsula and north-west Africa.

Habitat and Habits Found burrowing in sandy soil, often in the neighbourhood of watercourses, irrigated areas, and open woodland where it is both diurnal and nocturnal.

Housing An aquarium tank half filled with a mixture of sand, sterilised loam, and various sized pebbles with a few clumps of grass planted at the surface. The substrate should be sprayed with water two or three times per week to keep it slightly damp. It is best to limit the spraying to one area (ie the front half) so that the reptiles have a choice of dampness.

Heating and Lighting General substrate temperature around 25°C with supplementary lighting only necessary for plants.

Feeding Small insects, including ants. These will have to be sprinkled on the surface of the substrate and left for the reptiles to eat.

Community Best kept together with its own species. Other species of amphisbaenians require similar husbandry. One interesting method of keeping them is to have the substrate between two sheets of glass about 5cm (2in) apart and with a wooden frame around the edges. The animals can then be viewed in their burrows.

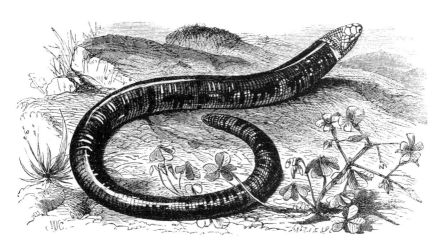

Sooty amphisbaenian

7·SNAKES OF THE WORLD

FAMILY: Blind Snakes—Typhlopidae—

This is a family of primitive burrowing snakes in which the scales are uniform on both the ventral and dorsal surfaces. The eyes are covered by enlarged scales and the mouth is extremely small, with teeth in the upper jaw only. They probably feed, day or night, on subterranean invertebrates, including earthworms. There are approximately 200 species in 5 genera, distributed through Central and South America, Africa (including Madagascar), south-west Asia and Australia. Little is known about their captive husbandry, but they should probably be kept somewhat in the manner of the amphisbaenians.

FAMILY: Thread Snakes—Leptotyphlopidae

Similar to the preceding family, but slimmer. The teeth are present in the lower jaw only. There are about 50 species in 2 genera found in Central and South America, and Africa. Little is known about their captive husbandry but their habits are similar to the previous family.

FAMILY: Cylinder Snakes—Aniilidae

This family contains about 9 species in 3 genera found in South America, south-east Asia, and Sri Lanka. The body is cylindrical in shape and covered with smooth, uniform scales. There is no distinct neck, the head running straight into the body. The blunt tail is relatively short. Teeth are present on the upper and lower jaws, as well as on the palate. They burrow and feed, day or night, on invertebrates and small vertebrates. Little is documented on their captive husbandry.

FAMILY: Shieldtail Snakes—Uropeltidae

Another family of burrowing snakes with 8 genera and about 40 species found only in India and Ceylon. The smooth scales are somewhat larger on the ventral than on the dorsal surface. The body is cylindrical, and the tail short, ending in an enlarged shield. The head runs straight into the body with no distinct neck. The eyes are relatively small. The teeth are present on the upper and lower jaws. They feed day or night on subterranean invertebrates. Little is known of their captive husbandry.

FAMILY: Pythons—Boas—Boidae

Members of the family Boidae include some of the most spectacular reptiles and, as such, are popular terrarium subjects. There are about 90 species in 22 genera found throughout the warmer parts of the world. They range in size from dwarf burrowing species 30cm (12in) in length, to giants in excess of 10m (33ft). Most have a robust body and a relatively short tail with small, smooth, dorsal scales, and broad ventral scales forming a single row under the trunk, a double row under the tail. There is a well defined neck separating the broad head from the body. The mouth is large and the teeth numerous and recurved, situated in the upper and the lower jaw and on the palate. Most are constrictors, catching vertebrate prey in the mouth and suffocating it to death using pressure from the body coils.

There are 2 subfamilies, the Pythoninae (pythons) and the Boinae (boas), the former occurring in Africa, Asia and Australia, the latter in the Americas, Madagascar, with some burrowing forms in southern Europe, Africa and Asia. The Pythoninae are oviparous, many of them actively incubating their stacks of eggs by coiling around them and increasing the body temperature to several degrees above the air temperature; the Boinae are ovo-viviparous.

Papuan Green Tree Python or Jamomong *Chondropython viridis*
Subfamily: Pythoninae
Length: 1.6m (5¼ft)

Description This species bears a remarkable resemblance to the emerald tree boa, *Corallus caninus*, considering they are in different subfamilies and live in widely separated continents. The body is laterally flattened and the broad head set off by a relatively narrow neck. The basic colour is leaf green with a yellow or white vertebral stripe, broken at intervals.
Range New Guinea and Solomon Islands.
Habitat and Habits A mainly nocturnal and strictly arboreal, rain forest inhabitant. When at rest it drapes its body symmetrically over a branch.
Housing A large tall terrarium with strong, climbing branches. Substrate of medium shingle with potted creeping plants such as *Philodendron* sp.

Heating and Lighting Daytime temperature around 28°C, reduced to around 22°C at night. Large aquarium heater in pool, aerator and infra-red lamp. Broad spectrum lighting; high humidity.
Feeding Mice, rats and birds.
Community Good with other species.
Colour Plate No: 19.

Carpet Python and Diamond Python *Morelia spilotes*
Subfamily: Pythoninae
Length: 3m (9¾ft)

Description There are two well documented subspecies, the diamond python, *M.s. spilotes*, and the carpet python *M.s. variegata*. The former is glossy black, with yellow diamond shaped spots, the latter variegated in shades of brown, buff and grey. The underside of both is yellowish, marked with grey. They are relatively slim snakes in spite of their considerable length.
Range Continental Australia with the exception of the western quarter. Also found in New Guinea.
Habitat and Habits A wide range of habitat from forest to scrub, or near desert. May be arboreal or terrestrial depending on the habitat. It hunts by day or night.
Housing A roomy terrarium with ample climbing facilities and a large water bath. Planting unnecessary. Gravel or concrete substrate with good washing down facilities.
Heating and Lighting Air temperature around 27°C, dropped to 22°C at night. Aquarium heaters (protected) in water bath. Infra-red lamps or, possibly, central heating with air convection. Fluorescent lighting; medium to high humidity.
Feeding Mice, rats and chicks.
Community Best kept alone or in true pairs.

Indian or Tiger Python *Python molurus*
Subfamily: Pythoninae
Length: 5m (16½ft)

Description There are two well documented subspecies, the light phase Indian python, *P. m. molurus*, and the dark phase Indian or Burmese python, *P. m. bivittatus*. The latter is the one most often available. The colour is a rich bronze brown, marked with a network of broad cream and buff bands. The former is similarly marked but altogether lighter in colour.
Range India, Ceylon, Burma, Indo-China, Malaysia and Indonesia.
Habitat and Habits Forested areas, particularly near water. Mainly

The royal python, *Python regius*, from West Africa

nocturnal; they are good climbers and swimmers and become remarkably tame in captivity.

Housing A roomy terrarium furnished with climbing branches and a large water bath. Substrate of large grade shingle, or shaped concrete. They need good washing down and drainage facilities.

Heating and Lighting Preferably central heating with warm air convection. Alternatively, electric heaters protected behind wire mesh. Daytime temperature around 28°C, cooler at night. Fluorescent lighting, high humidity.

Feeding Young specimens: mice; larger specimens: rats or small chickens; very large specimens: dead rabbits or large chickens.

Community Good with similar sized specimens. Males may injure each other during combat, therefore a close watch should be kept during mating activities, when more than one male is present.

Colour Plate No: 20.

Royal Python *Python regius*
Subfamily: Pythoninae
Length: 1.5m (5ft)

Description This is a popular terrarium subject due to its relatively small size and docility — even newly captured specimens hardly ever attempt to bite. Typically python shaped, it has a dark brown skin, broken with large irregular blotches of cream, or yellowish-buff.

Range West Africa.

Habitat and Habits Found in the tropical rain forest. Although it is a good climber, it tends to remain near ground level amongst the roots of trees and low vegetation. Its habit of rolling itself into a ball, with its head inside its coils when threatened, gives rise to its alternative name of ball python. Mainly nocturnal.

Housing As for other python species, but smaller.

Heating and Lighting Daytime temperature around 30°C, lowered to about 24°C at night. Aquarium heaters in pool; infra-red lamps. Broad spectrum lighting; high humidity.

Feeding Newly captured specimens are often difficult to entice into taking their first meal. One method worth trying is to place the snake into a secured bag containing a dead mouse; often the mouse will be eaten during the night.

Community Good with snakes of similar size and habit.

Reticulated Python *Python reticulatus*
Subfamily: Pythoninae
Length: 6m (20ft)

Description The longest of all snakes — though perhaps not as heavy as the anaconda. Exceptions to the average length given above include specimens in excess of 10m (33ft). The ground colour is light to dark brown with a reticulated pattern of black, yellow, and buff along the back. There is a double row of triangular to diamond shaped white patches along the flanks.

Range South-east Asia.

Habitat and Habits Mainly an inhabitant of the forest, usually close to stretches of water. Sometimes enters villages to rob poultry houses; it is known to take dogs and other domestic animals. Mainly nocturnal, it is an excellent climber and swimmer. Wild specimens have a reputation for being aggressive and can give a nasty bite. Large, newly captured specimens should always be handled by at least two people. Captive specimens reared from young make the best terrarium inmates.

Housing Before obtaining a specimen, ensure that space has been allowed for its growth. There always seems to be an excess of large pythons which have outgrown their homes. Housing should be as described for other python species, with an extra large, heated bath.

Heating and Lighting As for *P. molurus*.

Feeding Young specimens: mice and small rats. Large specimens: dead rabbits, chickens, ducks, or even turkeys.

Community Never keep more than one male together with females, unless a very close watch can be kept on the proceedings.

Colour Plate No: 21.

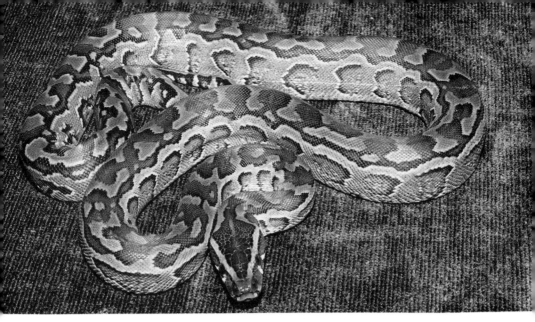

The African python, *Python sebae*, has a reputaton for being slightly more aggressive than its close relative the Indian Python, *P. molurus*

African Rock Python *Python sebae*
Subfamily: Pythoninae
Length: 5m (16½ft)

Description This species is very similar to *P. molurus* in form, size and colour; indeed, cross-breeding between the two species is not unknown. Colours are similar but somewhat darker and the pattern is different.

Range Many parts of Africa south of the Sahara.

Habitat and Habits Less of a forest inhabitant than *P. molurus*, it is found in savannah land, open woodland and rocky escarpments — often near to water where it is mainly nocturnal. Somewhat more aggressive than the Indian python, though captive reared specimens are reasonably tame if handled regularly.

Housing As described for *P. molurus*.

Heating and Lighting As described for *P. molurus*.

Feeding As described for *P. molurus*.

Community Young specimens are reasonably tolerant with snakes of similar size, but older specimens are best kept singly outside of the breeding season.

Boa constrictor *Boa constrictor*
Subfamily: Boinae
Length: 3m (10ft)

Description Contrary to common belief, this species is not such a giant when compared with other boids; however, specimens with a length

of 4m (13ft) have been known. It is a robust snake with a broad, triangular head, set off from the body by a narrower neck. Colour shows great variation through their range but is normally cream-buff with large uneven, but distinct, blotches of dark brown, which become progressively more reddish-brown towards the tail. In some specimens, the tail markings are almost pure red (thus: red-tailed boa).
Range Central and South America.
Habitat and Habits In the wild this species prefers dry areas of open woodland, rocky slopes and scrubland. It is an excellent climber but tends to avoid water. Adult specimens are untrustworthy and should be handled with care as they can give an unpleasant bite. Mainly nocturnal.
Housing A large terrarium with strong climbing branches and rock ledges. Substrate of large grade gravel or shaped concrete. A large water bath.
Heating and Lighting Daytime temperature around 28°C, reduced to about 20°C at night. Preferably central heating and air convection, otherwise electric heaters, or lamps protected with wire mesh. Fluorescent lighting; medium humidity.
Feeding Will live satisfactorily on a staple diet of rats. Youngsters to be fed on mice or day old chicks.
Community Best kept singly outside of the breeding season.
Colour Plate No: 22.

Rainbow Boa *Epicrates cenchria*
Subfamily: Boinae
Length: 2.5m (8¼ft)

Description Two varieties are known, one of which is plain tan in colour with a lighter underside, the other is marked with dark rings, which are lighter in the centre. However, all show a beautiful bloom, particularly when freshly sloughed and the various rainbow colours show themselves under certain light conditions. The body is fairly slender, more so in the males than in the females.
Range Northern South America.
Habitat and Habits Mainly found in wooded areas where it is an excellent climber. This species has a reliably stable temperament and is a popular subject for the terrarium. Mainly nocturnal.
Housing A medium sized terrarium with medium gravel substrate and a large water bath. Adequate climbing branches and as this snake is reasonably gentle in its movements, an attempt to grow robust plants (such as *Monstera* sp) may prove advantageous.
Heating and Lighting Daytime temperature about 28°C, reduced to 22°C at night. Aquarium heaters in water bath; infra-red lamps.

Fluorescent lighting; medium to high humidity.

Feeding Mice, rats and chicks.

Community Good with snakes of similar size and habit. Other species in the genus, such as the Haitian boa, *Epicrates striatus*, require similar husbandry.

Indian Sand Boa *Eryx johnii*
Subfamily: Boinae
Length: 85cm (33in)

Description A cylindrical shaped snake with a very short tail, which is the same shape as the head. The colour is a fairly uniform, sandy brown.

Range South central Asia.

Habitat and Habits Sandy, semi-desert and scrub areas where it is active by day or night. When threatened this species can burrow quickly under the sand. If this is not immediately possible, it raises its tail and moves it about as though it were the head.

Housing A low, semi-desert type terrarium with a substrate of coarse sand to a depth of 20cm (8in). One or two succulent plants can be grown in a separate floor area.

Heating and Lighting Ground temperature to 30°C during the day. Heat pad or cable, turned off at night. Supplementary lighting for benefit of plants. Low humidity.

Feeding Small mice and lizards. Shallow water container.

Community Best kept in single pairs. Other species in the genus, such as the rough-tailed sand boa, *E. conicus*, and the European sand boa, *E. jaculus*, require similar husbandry.

Anaconda *Eunectes murinus*
Subfamily: Boinae
Length: 6m (20ft)

Description The world's largest snake with the exception of *Python reticulatus*. Specimens in excess of 8m (26¼ft) have been recorded. Heavier in build than the other giant, some specimens may have a central body diameter in excess of 30cm (12in). The head is relatively narrow and the neck thick. The colour is olive green marked with dark brown, almost circular, blotches down the back. Along the flanks, similar blotches have a light buff centre. The eyes and the nostrils are set on top of the head, which indicate its semi-aquatic habitat.

Range Northern South America.

Habitat and Habits Mainly nocturnal, it lives in the rain forests and river systems of the Amazon and Orinoco basins. Never far from water, it is an excellent swimmer and preys on aquatic and amphibious animals ranging from fish and caiman, to ducks and capybaras.

Housing An extremely large, preferably brick built, terrarium, with built in heated pool to a depth of at least 60cm (23½in). Concrete or heavy shingle substrate with adequate washing down and drainage facilities. Strongly anchored climbing branches. Rock ledges.

Heating and Lighting Due to its huge bulk, the anaconda takes a long time to reach optimum temperature and a mistake often made is to have an unheated pool in which the snake will never quite become warm enough to feed properly. A circulatory waterfall, with the water passing through a thermostatically controlled immersion heater tank to keep the water temperature at not less than 25°C, is probably the best solution. Air temperature of 28°C, preferably by central heating, with little cooling at night; fluorescent lighting; high humidity.

Feeding Small specimens: fish, mice or rats; larger specimens, chickens, ducks or rabbits.

Community Best kept singly outside of the breeding season.

Rosy boa *Lichanura roseofusca*
Subfamily: Boinae
Length: 80cm (31½in)

Description A sturdily built small boa with a small oval head and a relatively short tail. The ground colour is bluish-grey and there are three longitudinal reddish-brown or pinkish, broken stripes along the dorsal surface.

Range Southern California and northern Mexico.

Habitat and Habits Found in rocky ravines, scrubland and open woodland. It is mainly terrestrial but is an accomplished climber. Nocturnal.

Housing A medium sized terrarium with coarse sand and leaf litter substrate, with a climbing branch and one or two sturdy plants.

Heating and Lighting Average daytime temperature around 25°C, cooler at night. Aquarium heater in water dish. Infra-red lamp; medium humidity, with lighting for the benefit of the plants only.

Feeding Small mice and chicks.

Hibernation A short, winter rest period at reduced temperature is recommended.

Community May be kept with species of similar size and habit.

FAMILY: Sunbeam Snake—Xenopeltidae

The single species in this family, the sunbeam snake, *Xenopeltis unicolor*, is found in southern India and south-east Asia. It has small dorsal scales and much enlarged ventral scales. A small head is joined to the cylindrical body with no obvious neck region and the tail is relatively short. The colour is a deep bronze to black, with a multi-coloured bloom, giving it a most attractive appearance. It is a burrowing snake which feeds primarily on small vertebrates. Little is known about its captive husbandry.

FAMILY: Wart or Elephant's Trunk Snakes—Acrochordidae

There are 2 genera, each with a single species in this unusual family. They are almost totally aquatic, living in tidal rivers and estuaries ranging from eastern India, through south-east Asia to northern Australia. The body scales are small and granular, both on the dorsal and ventral surfaces, and the skin hangs loosely on the trunk. The broad head is distinct from the body and the tail is relatively short and somewhat prehensile. The teeth are situated in the upper and lower jaws. They feed predominantly on fish.

Javan Wart Snake *Acrochordus javanicus*
Family: Acrochordidae
Length: 1.5m (5ft)

Description This species has small granular scales all over the body which is a light, creamy-brown in colour with a marbling of darker brown; the underside is white.
Range Coastal areas from Malaysia to northern Australia.
Habitat and Habits A sluggish snake, usually lying amongst submerged vegetation or tree roots, occasionally bringing its head to the surface to take in air. It is almost helpless if placed on dry land. Hunts by day or night.
Housing Must be kept in an aquarium with a minimum water depth of 25cm (10in). Gravel substrate, tree roots and rocks for decoration.
Heating and Lighting Aquarium heaters to maintain constant temperature of around 25°C. Supplementary lighting unnecessary unless plants are to be grown.
Feeding Various live fish.
Community Best kept singly as it seems to be bad tempered with members of its own species. Very little is documented on the breeding habits of this species.

FAMILY: Typical Snakes (Colubrines)—Colubridae

Colubrines are typically long, slender, fast snakes and form by far the largest snake group with over 2,500 species in about 250 families which are distributed throughout the warmer parts of the world. The small, dorsal scales are overlapping, those. on the ventral surface large, and forming a single row, doubling up below the typically long tail. Most species have relatively large eyes with round pupils. The numerous recurved teeth are borne on the upper and lower jaws, and, in most cases, on the palate. The subfamily Boiginae possess grooved, venom carrying, enlarged teeth at the rear of the upper jaw. The family contains snakes ranging from the typical to the highly specialised and includes arboreal, terrestrial, semi-aquatic and burrowing species.

Green Whip Snake *Coluber viridiflavus*
Subfamily: Colubrinae
Length: 1.5m (5ft)

Description This is a very fast-moving species with a long, slender body, a long tail, and a head separated from the body by a narrow neck. The upper surface is dark blackish-green, sprinkled with dots of yellowish-green; the area between the scales is likewise green. The underside is usually olive green with darker markings.
Range Central Europe.
Habitat and Habits Sunny slopes with low vegetation, dry stone walls, hedgerows, vineyards and other plantations. Diurnal and mainly terrestrial.
Housing Large, low terrarium with small grade shingle substrate, a few rocks and a tree root, together with one or two potted plants.
Heating and Lighting Daytime temperature around 25°C, cooled to 18°C at night. Infra-red lamp or cable heater (local). Broad spectrum lighting; medium humidity.
Feeding Mainly lizard and frog feeders in the wild – adults can usually be persuaded to take mice. Juveniles are more difficult to feed unless lizards are available. Shallow water container.
Hibernation A short, winter rest period at reduced temperature is recommended.
Community Best kept alone except in breeding season. Several other species in the genus, including *C. algirus*, *C. gemonensis*, and *C. hippocrepis* require similar husbandry, but which should reflect their geographical habitat.
Colour Plate No: 23.

28 Puff adder, *Bitis arietans*. This much feared, highly venomous viper lives and breeds well in captivity. It is probably responsible for more snake bites in Africa than any other snake species

29 Copperhead, *Agkistrodan contortrix*; a colourful North American pit viper

30 Eyelash viper, *Bothrops schlegeli*. This South American tree viper comes in a variety of colour forms

31 Timber rattlesnake, *Crotalus horridus*. One of many species in the genus, it is more colourful than most – but is equally as dangerous

Southern Smooth Snake *Coronella girondica*
Subfamily: Colubrinae
Length: 70cm (27½in)

Description A slender snake with brown to reddish-brown ground colour broken by darker bands and spots.
Range Southern Europe, north-west Africa.
Habitat and Habits Diurnal, it prefers dry areas, edges of agricultural land, sunny slopes and heathland. Hides under flat stones or in burrows.
Housing A medium sized terrarium with sand, peat and leaf litter substrate; one or two grass clumps, flat stones and a potted plant.
Heating and Lighting Daytime temperature to 28°C, cooled to 22°C at night. Infra-red lamp and broad spectrum lighting; low to medium humidity.
Feeding Feeds mainly on lizards but may be trained to take mice.
Hibernation Short, winter rest period at reduced temperature is recommended.
Community Best kept in single pairs.

Indigo Snake *Drymarchon chorais*
Subfamily: Colubrinae
Length: 2m (6½ft)

Description The subspecies *D. c. couperi*, found in the eastern part of the species range, is much sought after by the terrarium keeper on account of its glossy blue-black colouration, and its docile captive temperament. It is protected in its native habitat but captive bred specimens are sometimes available. Other forms of this species are less spectacular in colour, ranging from dull olive green to brown. The underside may be tinged with red.
Range Southern USA, Central and South America.
Habitat and Habits Dry, sandy areas and scrubland. Seeks refuge in gopher burrows. Diurnal and largely terrestrial it may feed on other snakes in the wild as well as various invertebrates.
Housing A large terrarium with coarse sand and shingle substrate, a hollow log and a couple of gnarled branches.
Heating and Lighting Daytime temperature around 27°C, reduced to 22°C at night. Infra-red lamp, cable or pad heater in substrate (local). Broad spectrum lighting; low to medium humidity.
Feeding Will take mice, rats and day old chicks. Water dish required.
Hibernation A winter rest period of 6–8 weeks at about 15°C is recommended.
Community Best kept singly, except at breeding time.

Ringneck or Cricket-eating Snake *Eirenis rothi*
Subfamily: Colubrinae
Length: 30cm (12in)

Description This is a very small but interesting species. It is typically colubrine in shape in spite of its small size. Its basic colour is olive brown. There is a wide black band around the neck and a yellow band across the head, the remainder of which is black.
Range South central Asia.
Habitat and Habits A semi-burrowing snake, often found under flat stones and other objects. May be found in agricultural areas and plantations as well as in scrubland where it is active by day or night.
Housing A small glass terrarium, with no small escape holes or cracks. Medium and coarse sand substrate with one or two flat stones, a potted, succulent plant, or other low herbage.
Heating and Lighting Daytime temperature around 26°C, reduced to 20°C at night. Small pad heater (local). Broad spectrum lighting; low to medium humidity.
Feeding Crickets, locusts and other small invertebrates as well as regular vitamin/mineral supplement. Small shallow water dish.
Community Best kept with its own species.

Corn Snake *Elaphe guttata*
Subfamily: Colubrinae
Length: 1.1m (3½ft)

Description A popular snake amongst herpetologists — as well as with farmers as it often dwells on agricultural land eating rodent pests. The slender body is buff with a pinkish tinge. A series of large red blotches with black borders run down the back. A further row of smaller blotches runs down each flank.
Range Eastern USA.
Habitat and Habits Varied habitat ranging from woodland to agricultural land, and is often found in the neighbourhood of dwellings. May hide in rodent burrows. Crepuscular and mainly terrestrial, though it can climb well.
Housing A tall terrarium with climbing branches, a mixed sand and peat substrate, and a potted creeping plant.
Heating and Lighting Daytime air temperature around 25°C. Local floor temperature to 30°C. Heat lamp, cable or pad heater (local) with reduced temperature at night. Broad spectrum lighting; medium humidity.
Feeding Will live on mice. Shallow water dish.
Hibernation A short, winter rest period at lower temperature is recommended.

Community Good with snakes of similar size and habit.
Colour Plate No: 24.

Rat Snake *Elaphe obsoleta*
Subfamily: Colubrinae
Length: 1.4–1.9m (4½–6¼ft)

Description There are several subspecies, the best known being the Texas rat snake, *E. o. lindheimeri* and the yellow rat snake, *E. o. quadrivittata.* The former is almost black, with large reticulations in buff to yellow; the latter is yellow to olive yellow, with four darker lines running the length of the body. Other subspecies include the black rat snake, *E. o. obsoleta,* the Florida rat snake, *E. o. rossalleni* and the grey rat snake, *E. o. spiloides.* There are many intergrades and colour variations.
Range North America.
Habitat and Habits A wide range of habitat including woodland, scrub and cultivated areas. Welcomed by farmers as consumers of rodents, although they sometimes take the chicks of domestic poultry. Crepuscular and terrestrial, they are also accomplished climbers.
Housing As described for *E. guttata.*
Heating and Lighting As described for *E. guttata.*
Feeding Mice, chicks and rats. Shallow water container.
Hibernation A short, winter rest period at reduced temperature.
Community Good with snakes of similar size and habit. Many other species in this large genus make good terrarium subjects including: the Aesculapian snake (Europe), *E. longissima,* the four-lined snake (Europe), *E. quatuorlineata,* the leopard snake (Europe), *E. situla,* the Trans-Pecos rat snake (North America), *E. subocularis,* and the fox snake (North America), *Elaphe vulpina.*

Mud Snake *Farancia abacura*
Subfamily: Colubrinae
Length: 1.3m (4¼ft)

Description Although somewhat difficult to keep, this species is interesting and attractive, therefore well worth the extra effort. It has a relatively small, oval head and a robust body. The tail is relatively short and ends with a spinelike scale. The body is blue black, and the belly deep rose red, which breaks as bars into the flanks.
Range South-eastern USA.
Habitat and Habits A terrestrial snake, usually found in swampy areas. It often enters water in search of prey. Burrows into mossy hummocks and under tree roots. Nocturnal.

Housing An aqua-terrarium with roughly half land and half water. Land area with shingle substrate. One or two tree roots and potted, moisture loving plants.

Heating and Lighting Daytime temperature around 26°C, cooler at night. Aquarium heater in water. Broad spectrum lighting; high humidity.

Feeding Lives mainly on salamanders in the wild. Can be trained to take fish and mice which have had a salamander rubbed over them and may also take frogs.

Hibernation Short, winter rest period at reduced temperature.

Community Good with other species but the specialised environment precludes most.

King Snake *Lampropeltis getulus*
Subfamily: Colubrinae
Length: 1.4–1.8m   (4½–6ft)

Description There are several subspecies with variable markings including the Californian king snake, *L. g. californiae*, which is usually banded in black and white, though a striped form exists; the Florida king snake, *L. g. floridana*, which is brown to olive brown with yellow markings on the scales; the chain king snake, *L. g. getulus*, which is

These two illustrations show the remarkable variety of pattern to be found in the king snake *Lampropeltis getulus*. The Californian subspecies, *L. g. californiae*, may be commonly found in both the banded and the striped phases

banded in black and white, with the white bands joining at the flanks, forming a chainlike pattern; and the speckled king snake, *L. g. holbrooki*, which is black with fine yellow spots.
Range North America.
Habitat and Habits With such a great number of subspecies the range of habitat varies considerably and they are found in woodland to semi-desert, the borders of swampland, and agricultural areas. Viewed with favour as they include other snakes in their diet, even rattlesnakes. Diurnal.
Housing Similar to that described for *Elaphe guttata*.
Heating and Lighting Similar to that described for *E. guttata*.
Feeding Will take mice, rats and chicks. Shallow water dish.
Hibernation Short, winter rest period at reduced temperature is recommended.
Community Not recommended to be kept with other species.
Colour Plate No:25.

Milk Snake *Lampropeltis triangulum*
Subfamily: Colubrinae
Length: 1.1m (3½ft)

Description This species gets its common name from an old belief that it takes milk from the udders of cows. A handsome snake marked in broad bands of yellow and red, separated by narrower black bands.
Range North America.
Habitat and Habits A shy, retiring snake, spending most of its time under leaf litter, fallen timber, or in burrows. Prefers open woodland in hilly areas where it is both diurnal and nocturnal.
Housing A low, semi-humid terrarium with sand and peat mixture as substrate, one or two small, hollow branches and a potted plant.
Heating and Lighting Daytime temperature around 25°C, cooler at night. Heat lamp or heat cable. Broad spectrum lighting; medium humidity.
Feeding Lizards and snakes; can be trained to take small mice.
Hibernation Short period at lower temperature.
Community Best kept in single pairs.
Colour Plate No: 26.

Viperine Snake *Natrix maura*
Subfamily: Colubrinae
Length: 1m (3¼ft)

Description The thick body and triangular head of this species gives it a somewhat viperine appearance, hence its common name. Olive

Grass snake, *Natrix natrix*

brown or green in colour, with two rows of staggered, dark blotches down the back — sometimes forming a zig-zag pattern.

Range South-west Europe, north-west Africa.

Habitat and Habits Usually found in or near water, damp open woodland, or meadows. Often basks at water's edge and dives in if disturbed. Irritable when first captured but becomes reasonably tame in captivity. Diurnal.

Housing An aqua-terrarium with roughly half land and half water. Substrate of fine grade shingle with one or two tree roots or gnarled branches. Potted, moisture loving plants.

Heating and Lighting Water temperature to be maintained around 24°C with thermostatically controlled aquarium heater. Air temperature to 28°C, cooler at night. Infra-red lamp. Broad spectrum lighting; high humidity.

Feeding Fish, frogs and earthworms.

Hibernation Short, winter rest period at reduced temperature.

Community Good with its own species, or with snakes of similar size and habit. Other species in the genus, including the dice snake (Europe), *N. tesselata*, and the grass snake (Europe), *N. natrix*, require similar husbandry.

Northern Water Snake *Nerodia sipedon*
Subfamily: Colubrinae
Length: 1m (3¼ft)

Description A relatively slender watersnake with a long tail. The ground colour is brown to reddish-brown, which is marked by a number of darker, diagonal bands along the body.

Range Southern Canada, northern USA.

Habitat and Habits The banks of rivers, ponds and lakes — often entering the water in search of prey. Climbs into branches over-hanging water in order to bask. Diurnal and ovo-viviparous.

Housing As described for *Natrix maura*.

Heating and Lighting As described for *N. maura*.

Feeding Fish and frogs.

Hibernation Period of 8–10 weeks at a reduced temperature.

Community Good with snakes of similar size and habit. Several other species in the genus require similar husbandry including the red-bellied water snake (North America), *N. erythrogaster*, and the brown water snake (North America), *N. taxispilota*.

Pine snake *Pituophis melanoleucus*
Subfamily: Colubrinae
Length: 2m (6½ft)

Description This is a fairly robust species with a ground colour of creamy white. A row of large black blotches extends along the back, closer together at the anterior end than they are at the posterior. Further rows of smaller dark patches extend along the flanks.

Range Eastern USA.

Habitat and Habits Found in pine forests and related heathland where it is mainly diurnal.

Housing Large, tall terrarium with coarse sand substrate, decorated with a few pebbles, climbing branches preferably of pine and one or two potted plants.

Heating and Lighting Daytime air temperature around 25°C. Local basking temperature to 30°C. Heat lamp or cable heating (local). Broad spectrum lighting; medium humidity.

Feeding Mice, small rats and day old chicks. Small water container.

Hibernation Short, winter rest period at reduced temperature is recommended.

Community Outside of the breeding season they are best kept singly.

Asian Rat Snake *Ptyas mucosus*
Subfamily: Colubrinae
Length: 2–2.5m (6½–8¼ft)

Description A powerfully built colubrid which is olive brown with black spots on the scales, starting in the latter half of the body and forming faint diagonal bands.

Range Central, south and south-east Asia.

Habitat and Habits Dry scrubland areas. Mainly diurnal.

Housing Large, tall terrarium with substrate of sand and peat, decorated with a few pebbles, a large climbing branch and one or two robust potted plants.

Heating and Lighting Daytime air temperature to 28°C, local basking temperature to 30°C. Infra-red lamp or local cable heating. Broad spectrum lighting; medium humidity.

Feeding Mice, rats and day old chicks.

Hibernation A period of 8–10 weeks at reduced temperature is recommended.

Community Best kept singly, except when breeding.

Black and Yellow Rat Snake *Spilotes pullatus*
Subfamily: Colubrinae
Length: 3m (10ft)

Description A large, graceful snake with a relatively small head and a long, narrow tail. The body is laterally flattened and patterned in brilliant yellow and black.

Range Central and South America.

Habitat and Habits Diurnal and semi-arboreal, it is found in trees and shrubs, often close to water. Very irritable when first captured and shows its anger by spreading its neck vertically and repeatedly striking. Oviparous.

Housing A large, tall terrarium with shingle substrate and several stout climbing branches. Planting would be pointless as the snake will soon break them.

Heating and Lighting Air temperature to 30°C, cooler at night. Infra-red lamp; aquarium heater in water container. Broad spectrum lighting; high humidity.

Feeding Mice, rats and day old chicks. Large water container.

Community Best kept singly outside of the breeding season.

Garter Snake *Thamnophis sirtalis*
Subfamily: Colubrinae
Length: 60cm (24in)

Description Garter snakes are very popular terrarium subjects, being small, attractive, docile and relatively easy to feed. They are ideal for the beginner. It is a slender snake with a narrow head. The basic colour is brown to olive brown with three yellowish stripes running down the back. The colour is further broken by a series of squarish blotches running down the body between the stripes.

Range Eastern USA.

Habitat and Habits In damp areas, never far from water which it enters in search of prey. Diurnal.

Housing An aqua-terrarium, but with dry-basking areas and adequate ventilation. Small grade shingle as substrate with a few flat basking

The common garter snake, *Thamnophis sirtalis*, is probably the most popular of all pet snakes, being easy to feed and accommodate

stones, a small climbing branch and one or two potted plants.

Heating and Lighting Daytime air temperature 20–25°C, cooler at night. Small infra-red lamp or tungsten bulb. Aquarium heater in water. Broad spectrum lighting; high humidity.

Feeding Earthworms, small fish and strips of dead fish (but see Chapter 4).

Hibernation A hibernation period of 10–12 weeks is recommended.

Community Good with snakes of similar size and habit. There are several other species in the genus requiring similar husbandry.

VENOMOUS SNAKES

All venomous snakes, however mild the venom is reputed to be, should be treated with the utmost caution and respect. It is all very well to say that venomous snakes should not be kept in the home, but there will always be those persons who insist, or persist, in keeping them — hopefully for purely scientific and aesthetic interest, rather than for egotistical motives. People who keep such reptiles have a great responsibility, not only to the snakes and themselves, but also to their family and even their neighbours. In the UK, the USA and certain other countries, venomous reptiles may only be kept under licence, after the appropriate authorities are satisfied that the keeper is sensible and that all possible safety precautions have been taken to minimise the risk of venomous snakebits.

Before acquiring any venomous snake, one should ensure that one has suitable facilities and that the appropriate antivenene is available. The latter should be stored to the manufacturer's instructions (usually in a refrigerator) and one should ensure that a new stock is obtained before the old one is out of date. Information on suppliers of antivenene for the various species may be obtained through your herpetological society, or from the nearest zoo having venomous snakes.

All cases of snakebite should be referred immediately to a medical practitioner and, to this end, it is wise to ensure that your local doctor, or hospital, is aware of the details of the type of snakes kept, and the location of the antivenenes. Do-it-yourself treatment, such as incising the site of the bite, is an archaic practice and should not be attempted. If medical attention is not immediately available, a tourniquet may be applied to a limb, above the bite, but this should be loosened at intervals of not more than fifteen minutes to allow blood circulation. The patient must receive medical attention with all possible haste, but it is important to remain calm and not panic.

Venomous snakes must be kept in strongly built terraria, with access doors secured with two padlocks, which should be kept locked at all times except during routine maintenance of the cages. Terraria should be kept on a solid, stable surface, so that there is no danger of them falling and breaking open. Ideally, terraria should be kept in a locked room or outhouse — which has been thoroughly checked for potential escape routes. Ensure that adequate handling equipment is available, including snake sticks, grabs, trapping boxes, and thick leather gloves. A notice should be placed on the door of the snake room warning of its contents, and a further notice should be placed on each cage, giving the name of the species, the location of the appropriate antivenene, and the procedure to be taken in case of an emergency.

Long-nosed Tree Snake *Ahaetulla nasuta*
Subfamily: Colubrinae
Length: 1.5m (5ft)

Description A most bizarre looking snake, extremely long and thin, with a broad head leading into a long pointed snout. A groove runs from the front of the eye, which has horizontal pupils, and down the snout, giving this species the unique attribute of forward looking, binocular vision. The dorsal surface and flanks are coloured a uniform light green, whilst the underside is yellowish-white.
Range South-east Asia.
Habitat and Habits A truly arboreal species active by day or night, which, should it find itself on the ground, has some difficulty in

moving. It tends to lie amongst foliage with the front third of its body hanging in the air, often pulled into the shape of an S, ready to strike out at any small lizards or tree frogs which may approach. It is rear-fanged, docile, and rarely attempts to bite.

Housing A tall terrarium with humus substrate, climbing branches, and thick creeping plants.

Heating and Lighting Fairly constant temperature, daytime 28°C, night-time 24°C. Aquarium heater in water. Infra-red lamp. Broad spectrum lighting; high humidity.

Feeding Primarily a lizard and frog eater, but will take small fish (eg guppies) from a shallow dish of water. Droplet drinker, so foliage must be sprayed regularly.

Community Good with snakes of similar size and habit. The closely related green whip snake, *Ahaetulla prasina*, requires similar husbandry.

Mangrove Snake *Boiga dendrophila*
Subfamily: Boiginae
Length: 1.8m (6ft)

Description This is a spectacular and popular terrarium subject which is usually available. It is a strongly built snake with a glossy black body and a bright yellow underside, the colour breaking into the flanks of the laterally compressed body in a series of bars.

Range South-east Asia.

Habitat and Habits As its common name implies, it is commonly found in coastal and estuarine areas amongst the mangrove trees, as well as further inland in thick forest. Almost totally arboreal, it seems to dislike coming to the ground. It is nocturnal, rear-fanged and irritable.

Housing A tall, humid terrarium with strong climbing branches and robust potted plants. Medium grade shingle is best as a substrate.

Heating and Lighting As described for *Ahaetulla nasuta*.

Feeding Mice, small rats and day old chicks. The latter seem to be its favourite captive food. Large water container.

Community Best kept singly outside of the breeding season.

Colour Plate No: 27.

Golden Tree Snake *Chrysopelia ornata*
Subfamily: Boiginae
Length: 1.2m (4ft)

Description Sometimes called the 'flying snake', this species can launch itself from the end of tree branches and parachute some considerable distance by spreading its body so that the underside is concave. The body is yellowish-green, with a network of dark brown or black lines bordering the scales. A smaller black line is found in the centre of each scale.

Range South-east Asia.

Habitat and Habits Mainly nocturnal it is a truly arboreal species which is rear-fanged, though not generally considered dangerous – however, precaution is advised.

Housing A tall terrarium with adequate climbing branches and robust plants. Medium grade shingle for substrate.

Heating and Lighting As described for *Ahaetulla nasuta*.

Feeding A lizard and frog eater in the wild. Can be trained to take mice. Foliage should be sprayed regularly. Water dish.

Community Best kept in single pairs. The closely related paradise tree snake, *Chrysopelia paradisi*, requires similar husbandry.

Vine Snake *Oxybelis aeneus*
Subfamily: Boiginae
Length: 1.5m (5ft)

Description The body shape of this species is not dissimilar to that of *Ahaetulla nasuta*. The snout is long and spade shaped. The dorsal surface is bronze in colour, the underside yellow with a dark line dividing the two colours.

Range Central and South America.

Habitat and Habits A truly arboreal species found in forested areas. Rear-fanged, but not generally considered dangerous, though precaution is advised.

Housing As described for *Ahaetulla nasuta*.

Heating and Lighting As described for *A. nasuta*.

Feeding A lizard eater. May be trained to take small fish from a shallow water container. Foliage to be sprayed daily.

Community Good with snakes of similar size and habit. The closely related *A. fulgidus*, requires similar husbandry.

FAMILY: Cobras—Kraits—Mambas—Coral Snakes—Elapidae

This family contains about 180 species in 40 families distributed throughout the warmer parts of the world, but absent from Europe, Madagascar and New Zealand. The dorsal scales are small and overlapping, the ventrals are enlarged to form a single row. The head is usually broader than the neck, and many species have a resemblance to colubrids. Teeth are present on the upper and lower jaws and on the palate, and there is a pair of enlarged venom fangs at the front of the upper jaw. All species are poisonous, many danger-ously so. Most feed on small vertebrates.

Banded Krait *Bungarus fasciatus*
Family: Elapidae
Length: 1.5m (5ft)

Description The body of this species is triangular in section and the head relatively small and rounded. The tail is relatively short and blunt. It is vividly coloured in broad, dark brown and yellow bands along the body.
Range South-east Asia.
Habitat and Habits A terrestrial species found in a variety of habitats from cultivated areas to open woodland, and scrub. Nocturnal and highly venomous, but not normally aggressive. May be irritable during the slough, so special precaution is advised.
Housing A low type terrarium with medium shingle substrate, one or two rocks, and a catching box.
Heating and Lighting Optimum daytime temperature 28°C, cooler at night. Infra-red heater or local cable heating. Broad spectrum light-ing; medium humidity.
Feeding Feeds mainly on other snakes in the wild. In the absence of snakes this species must be force fed on fish or mice. Large, shallow water container for drinking and bathing.

Western Green Mamba *Dendroaspis viridis*
Family: Elapidae
Length: 1.8m (6ft)

Description The most attractive of the mambas, with a long slender body and a relatively narrow head. It is leaf green in colour, lighter on the underside, the skin between the scales being black.
Range West Africa.
Habitat and Habits This species is just as much at home on the ground as in the trees, but spends most of its time amongst the foliage. Found mainly in open woodland and wooded savannah. Highly venomous and fast moving; definitely not recommended for the beginner. Diurnal.
Housing A tall terrarium with adequate climbing branches. Substrate of medium shingle. For safety reasons it is best to leave out plants.
Heating and Lighting Optimum daytime temperature around 28°C, cooler at night. Cable or pad heater, or infra-red lamp. Fluorescent lighting; low to medium humidity.

Feeding Mice, rats and day old chicks. Large water container for drinking and bathing.

Community Best kept singly, unless breeding is contemplated. Other species in the genus, including the eastern green mamba, *D. angusticeps*, Jameson's mamba, *D. jamesoni*, and the black mamba, *D. polylepis*, require similar husbandry.

Indian Cobra *Naja naja*
Family: Elapidae
Length: 1.5m (5ft)

Description Like most cobras, this species rears the front third of its body and spreads a hood when angered. It is a robust snake, blue black in colour, with yellowish markings along the body. At the rear of the spread hood a distinct spectacle (western race), or monocle (eastern race) marking is usually present.

Range India and south-east Asia.

Habitat and Habits Wide range of habitat from wooded to open areas, gardens and plantations. Terrestrial, nocturnal, and very dangerous.

Housing Large terrarium, preferably with concrete floor and a large water bath with adequate washing down and drainage facilities. One or two tree stumps for decoration.

Heating and Lighting Daytime air temperature around 30°C, cooler at night. Heat lamps or floor heating (local). Fluorescent lighting; medium humidity.

Feeding Mice, rats and day old chicks. Large water container for drinking and bathing.

Community Good with those of its own species or size.

Indian cobra, *Naja naja*

FAMILY: Sea Snakes—Hydrophidae

A family of almost totally marine reptiles bearing close relationship to the Elapidae. There are approximately 50 species in 16 genera found in the warmer parts of the Indian and Pacific Oceans, some staying in coastal areas but others travelling far out to sea. Most are ovo-viviparous and do not require to come onto land to lay eggs. In the majority of species the head is relatively small, and the body and tail are laterally flattened to aid swimming. Due to their specialised requirements they are rarely kept in captivity, other than in a large public aquarium. They are all highly venomous.

FAMILY: Vipers—Pit Vipers—Viperidae

The most highly advanced of all snakes, there are some 150 species in 14 genera broken into 2 well defined subfamilies. The Viperinae, or true vipers, are widely distributed throughout Africa and Asia; the Crotalinae, or pit vipers, throughout the Americas and parts of Asia. The latter possess heat sensitive pits between the eye and the nostril, which are used to detect warm-blooded prey. All viperids have relatively small scales on the dorsal surface, and enlarged ventral scales forming a single row under the body — breaking into a double row under the tail. The head is broad and the neck relatively narrow. Teeth are present on the upper and lower jaws and on the palate. A pair of erectile venom fangs are situated at the front of the upper jaw. All are venomous, many dangerously so. Most are ovo-viviparous but some lay eggs.

Rough-scaled Bush Viper *Atheris hispidus*
Subfamily: Viperinae
Length: 50cm (19½in)

Description This little viper has a slender body, small head and large eyes. The scales stand out from the body, giving it an almost hairy appearance. The basic colour is olive green, marked with a series of dark spots and blotches.
Range East Africa.
Habitat and Habits An arboreal species found in shrubs and low vegetation. Nocturnal and venomous, but not considered highly dangerous; however, treat with respect.
Housing A tall terrarium with climbing branches and potted plants. Substrate of sand, peat and leaf litter.
Heating and Lighting Optimum daytime temperature around 26°C,

Rough-scaled bush viper, *Atheris hispidus*. The extraordinary scales of this small viper give it an almost 'hairy' appearance (*Dave Barker, Dallas*)

cooler at night. Infra-red lamp or local cable heating. Broad spectrum lighting; low to medium humidity.

Feeding Normally feeds on lizards, frogs and nestling birds, but may be trained to take small mice.

Community Best kept in single pairs.

Puff Adder *Bitis arietans*
Subfamily: Viperinae
Length: 1.1m (3½ft)

Description A stout snake with large triangular head and a short tail. Colour is variable from olive brown to almost black — with a series of creamy white chevrons along the back.

Range Most of Africa south of the Sahara with the exception of rain forest areas.

Habitat and Habits Active by day or night it is found in dry savannah and semi-desert where its pattern acts as excellent camouflage. An irritable, highly dangerous snake which should only be kept by experienced herpetologists.

Housing Large low terrarium with medium gravel substrate and a few flat stones.

Heating and Lighting Daytime temperature to 30°C, basking area to 35°C. Heat lamp and local cable or pad heater. Broad spectrum lighting; low humidity.

Feeding Mice, rats and day old chicks. Large water container for drinking and bathing.

Community Best kept with its own species. Tolerant. Other species in the genus, such as the Gaboon viper, *B. gabonica*, and the rhinoceros viper, *B. nasicornis*, require similar husbandry but with medium to high humidity.
Colour Plate No: 28.

Desert Horned Viper *Pseudocerastes persicus*
Subfamily: Viperinae
Length: 60cm (24in)

Description A small, slender snake with a pointed horn above each eye. The ground colour is sandy buff with alternating squarish patches of dark brown down the back.
Range Middle East.
Habitat and Habits Inhabits scrubland and semi-desert. Crepuscular, hiding in rodent burrows or under rocks during the hotter part of the day. Venomous.
Housing A low, desert type terrarium with substrate of coarse sand and a few rocks, with one or two potted succulent plants.
Heating and Lighting Optimum daytime temperature around 30°C, reduced to 20°C at night. Infra-red lamp or pad heater (local). Broad spectrum lighting; low humidity.
Feeding Small mice. Shallow water dish.
Community Best kept in single pairs.

Nose-horned Viper *Vipera ammodytes*
Subfamily: Viperinae
Length: 90cm (35½in)

Description For its size, a fairly robust snake. There is a soft, hornlike appendage on the top of the snout between the nostrils. The grey-brown skin has a zig-zag stripe of reddish-brown bordered with black along the back. There is a further series of dark patches along each flank.
Range South-eastern Europe and south-west Asia.
Habitat and Habits Heathland, scrubland, rocky, and stony areas where it hides in burrows and under rocks. Diurnal. Venomous; handle with care.
Housing As described for *Pseudocerastes persicus*.
Heating and Lighting As described for *P. persicus*.
Feeding Mice and day old chicks. Shallow water dish.
Hibernation Short, winter rest period at lower temperature is recommended.
Community Best kept alone or in single pairs.

Adder or Northern Viper *Vipera berus*
Subfamily: Viperinae
Length: 70cm (27½in)

Description A slender viper, usually off-white in colour with a brown zig-zag stripe along the back in females, black in the males.
Range Central and northern Europe and Asia.
Habitat and Habits Diurnal, it is found in heathland, open woodland, moor and semi-tundra. Venomous; should be treated with respect.
Housing Best suited to outdoor reptiliary.
Feeding Mainly lizards but may sometimes take mice or voles.
Heating and Lighting In terrarium, basking areas to 30°C, cooler at night. Heat lamp. Broad spectrum lighting; medium humidity.
Hibernation A full hibernation period of 12–16 weeks is recommended.
Community Should only be kept in pairs in the terrarium. Greater numbers may be kept together in the reptiliary.

Water moccasin, *Agkistrodon piscivorus*

Copperhead *Agkistrodon contortrix*
Subfamily: Crotalinae
Length: 80cm (31½in)

Description This pit viper has a triangular head and a plump body. The basic colours are buff and bronze in alternating irregular sized bands along the body.
Range Eastern USA.
Habitat and Habits Dry, open woodland, scrubland and rocky slopes. Crepuscular. Venomous; should be treated with care.
Housing A large, low terrarium with medium gravel substrate and one or two rocks.
Heating and Lighting Average 25°C daytime temperature, lower at night. Heat lamp or cable heater (local). Broad spectrum lighting; medium humidity.
Feeding Mice, small rats, and day old chicks.
Hibernation Short, winter rest period at reduced temperature is recommended.
Community Best kept singly, unless breeding is contemplated. Other species in the genus, including the cantil (Mexico), *A. bilineatus*; the Malayan mocassin (S.E. Asia), *A. rhodostoma*, and the water mocassin (USA), *A. piscivorus*, require similar husbandry, depending on their wild habitat.
Colour Plate No: 29.

Eyelash Viper *Bothrops schlegeli*
Subfamily: Crotalinae
Length: 70cm (27½in)

Description This small tree viper comes in a wide variety of colours ranging from yellow, through green, to almost black with a number of different combinations.
Range Central and South America.
Habitat and Habits Found amongst the foliage of trees and shrubs where it is mainly nocturnal. Venomous; handle with care.
Housing A tall terrarium with climbing branches and one or two robust potted plants. Substrate of peat, sand and leaf litter.
Heating and Lighting Average temperature of 26°C, with little variation. Aquarium heaters in water. Heat lamp. Broad spectrum lighting; high humidity.
Feeding Frogs and small mice. Large water container together with regular spraying of foliage.
Community Good with snakes of similar size and habit, but for safety reasons best kept in single pairs.
Colour Plate No: 30.

Western diamondback rattlesnake, *Crotalus atrox*. This aggressive and dangerous species should only be kept by licenced and experienced herpetologists

Western Diamondback Rattlesnake *Crotalus atrox*
Subfamily: Crotalinae
Length: 1.5m (5ft)

Description A large, heavily built snake with a rattle at the tip of the tail consisting of loose rings of horny tissue. The basic colour is sandy brown, or grey, marked with a series of white diamonds down the back. The tail below the rattle is marked with vivid black and white bands.

Range Western USA.

Habitat and Habits Dry prairie, rocky areas and scrubland with sparse vegetation. Hides in rodent burrows. Diurnal. Highly venomous; not recommended for beginners.

Housing Large, low terrarium with sand and gravel substrate, rocks for decoration and one or two potted cacti.

Heating and Lighting Air temperature around 26°C, local basking temperature to 35°C. Heat lamp or cable heater (local). Broad spectrum lighting; low humidity.

Feeding Mice, small rats and day old chicks.

Community Best kept alone or in single pairs. Other species in the genus require similar husbandry.

Colour Plate No: 31 – related species.

APPENDIX:
Herpetological Societies

It is in the interests of all keepers, or prospective keepers, of captive reptiles to join a local or national herpetological society. It is only by constant contact with other herpetologists — through meetings, journals, newsletters, or correspondence — that one can keep up to date with the latest trends in husbandry. Most countries have a herpetological society but as most of these have amateur status addresses change frequently, therefore with two exceptions, it has not been considered practicable to include addresses in the following list. Addresses can be obtained by enquiring at libraries, pet shops, or zoos. The reptile departments of major zoos and museums will usually be pleased to give information by correspondence or over the phone.

UK: The Association for the Study of Reptilia and Amphibia (ASRA), c/o Cotswold Wild Life Park, Burford, Oxon, England. Publications: *ASRA Journal* (sporadically) and *Rephiberary* (monthly).

British Herpetological Society, c/o Zoological Society of London, Regent's Park, London NW1, England. Publications: *British Journal of Herpetology* and *BHS Bulletin* (two of each per annum).

International Herpetological Society. Publications: *The Herptile* (four per annum) and newsletters.

Europe: Societas Europaea Herpetologica (European Herpetological Society). Publications: *Amphibia-Reptilia* (four per annum). May be ordered direct from the publishers: Akademische Verlagsgesellschaft, Postfach 1107, D-6200 Wiesbaden, German Federal Republic.

Deutsche Gesellschaft für Herpetologie und Terrarienkunde. Publications: *Salamandra* (four per annum) and newsletters.

Nederlandse Vereniging voor Herpetologie en Terrariumkunde. Publications: *Lacerta* (twelve per annum).

USA: Herpetologists' League. Publication: *Herpetologica* (four per annum).

Society for the Study of Amphibians and Reptiles (SSAR). Publications: *Herpetological Review*, *Journal of Herpetology* (four of each per annum). SSAR produces regular reprints of herpetological classics and other interesting items.

Africa: Herpetological Association of Africa. Publication: *Journal of the Herpetological Association of Africa* (two per annum).

Asia: Japanese Herpetological Society. Publication: *Japanese Journal of Herpetology* (four per annum).

Australia and New Zealand: The Australian and New Zealand Herpetological Societies produce a joint journal, *Herpetofauna* (two per annum), plus individual newsletters.

GLOSSARY

In addition to many zoological terms used in this book, the following glossary contains explanations of other words which may be of use to the herpetologist.

Acrodont With teeth fused to the summit of the jawbones.
Aestivation The period of inactivity taken by many species during the dry season in tropical climates.
Agar A mucilaginous substance extracted from seaweeds and used as a gelling agent.
Aglyphous Appertaining to snakes which possess no venom fangs.
Albumen The white protein part of an egg.
Allanto-chorion An embryonic membrane.
Allantois A sac in the developing egg which primarily functions as a vessel for waste products.
Allopatric A condition in which different species do not inhabit the same area.
Amnion The membrane enclosing the amniotic cavity.
Amniotic cavity An enclosed, fluid-filled sac, protecting the embryo in reptiles, birds and mammals.
Anal gland A paired gland, situated at the base of the tail in many snakes and evacuating into the vent. They produce a foul smelling fluid used in defence when the reptile is attacked.
Anapsid An absence of temporal openings in the skull roof.
Anterior Appertaining to the front part of the body.
Antivenene Serum produced to combat the effects of (snake) venom.
Aorta The primary artery carrying blood away from the heart.
Aposematic Being marked with gaudy, contrasting colours as a warning to aggressors that the potential victim is venomous or noxious.
Arboreal Predominantly tree dwelling.
Arcade Parts of the skull roof separating the orbits and the temporal openings.
Autotomy The voluntary shedding of parts of the body in animals, usually in defence. Autotomy of the tail is common in many lizard species.
Binomial The system of double naming in scientific nomenclature using generic and trivial names to indicate a species.
Brill The transparent immovable spectacle covering the eye in snakes and some lizards.
Broad spectrum In this book, used in the context of terrarium lighting apparatus which emits light as near as possible to the quality of natural daylight.
Buccal cavity The cavity of the mouth.
Carpals The bones of the wrist in tetrapods.
Cerebellum The large paired lobe of the hind brain.

Cerebrum The lobes of the forebrain.

Cervical vertebrae The bones of the neck.

Chorion The outer membrane enclosing the embryo in higher vertebrates.

Classification The cataloguing of living things into systematic groups.

Cleidoic An egg which is protected from the atmosphere by an impervious shell.

Cloaca The chamber in many vertebrates into which the contents of the alimentary, urinary and reproductive systems discharge.

Condyle The rounded part of a bone fitting into the socket of another to form a joint.

Constriction A method used by some snakes to overpower prey which uses the application of pressure from the coils to cause asphyxia.

Convergence The similarity in form of unrelated organisms due to evolutionary development in similar habitats.

Cranium The bony part of the skull enclosing the brain.

Crepuscular Being mainly active during the twilight hours (dusk and dawn).

Cutaneous Appertaining to the skin.

Cytology The study of cell structure.

Dentary The anterior tooth bearing bone of the lower jaw.

Dermis The inner layer of skin.

Diapsid The condition of the skull which possesses two temporal openings.

Display A ritualised pattern of behaviour directed at other animals for sexual, territorial, or protective motives.

Diurnal Being mainly active during the hours of daylight.

Dorsal Referring to the upper side of the body.

Ecdysis The periodic shedding (sloughing) of the outer epidermal layer in lizards and snakes.

Ecosystem The complete environment in which an animal lives. Composed of living and non-living entities together with the elements.

Ectoparasite A parasite which attaches itself to the outer part of the body in order to extract nourishment from its host (eg ticks, mites).

Ectothermic A condition in which body heat is derived from external sources such as solar radiation (*also*: poikilothermic, coldblooded).

Endoparasite A parasite which derives nourishment from its host from the inner part of the body.

Endothermic A condition in which the body heat is maintained at more or less constant temperature, as exhibited in birds and mammals (*also* homoiothermic, warmblooded).

Epidermis The outer layer of skin.

Fang A large specialised tooth adapted for the injection of poison into prey.

Femur The main bone of the hind limb extending from the knee to the pelvis.

Femoral pores A number of hollow scales arranged on the underside of the thighs in many lizards. Usually better developed in males, they can be used in some species as a means of sex identification. Their function is not understood.

Foramen magnum The opening at the base of the skull which allows the spinal cord to connect to the brain.

Hemipenes The paired sex organ of the male, typical in lizards and snakes.

Herpetology The study of amphibians and reptiles.

Herptile A name used to collectively describe an amphibian or reptile.

Herptiliary An outside enclosure used for keeping both amphibians and reptiles in near natural conditions.

Heterodont Possessing teeth of several types (eg tearing, cutting, crushing, grinding).

Hibernation The act of spending the cold winter months in a state of torpor.

Hibernaculum A winter retreat in which to hibernate (*pl* hibernacula).

Homodont Possessing teeth of a single type.

Humerus The main bone of the forelimb extending from the elbow to the pectoral girdle.

Hybrid The usually sterile young produced as a result of a cross mating between two different species.

Hypervitaminosis A nutritional disorder caused by an over abundance of a certain vitamin(s) in the diet.

Hypovitaminosis A nutritional disorder caused by a deficiency of a certain vitamin(s) in the diet.

Intergrade An animal which may show the mixed characteristics of two different subspecies at the border of their respective ranges.

Jacobson's organ A pair of organs situated in the anterior part of the palate corresponding with and closely allied to the internal nares. Used to smell the contents of the mouth and may be used in conjunction with the forked tongue.

Kinesis The ability of a lizard to raise the upper part of the skull through movement of the quadrate.

Labial Appertaining to the lips.

Larynx The upper part of the trachea containing the vocal cords.

Ligament Non-elastic bone connecting tissue.

Liquid paraffin Liquid petroleum used as a mild laxative – known in the USA as mineral oil.

Mandible The lower jaw.

Maxilla The marginal, tooth bearing bone at the front of the upper jaw.

Medulla The section of the brain linking the spinal cord with the higher centres.

Melanism A condition in which an animal possesses an unusually abundant amount of dark pigment in the skin such as to make it appear black. Fairly common in certain lizard and snake species.

Metacarpals The middle bones of the hand (forefoot), between the phalanges and carpals.

Metatorsals The middle bones of the foot, between the torsals and the phalanges in the hind limb.

Montane Mountain dwelling.

Morphology The study of form, especially in relation to appearance, anatomy and development of animals.

Neural canal The canal in the vertebral column through which the spinal cord passes.

Nictitating membrane Sometimes known as the 'third eyelid', a delicate membrane capable of being drawn across the eye.

Nocturnal Mainly active during the hours of darkness.

Ocelli Spots resembling eyes occurring in the skin patterns of reptiles, especially lizards (*ocellated*: with eye spots).

Oesophagus The part of the alimentary canal anterior to the stomach.

Opistoglyphous Appertaining to snakes with grooved poison fangs at the rear of the jaw (*also*: back-fanged, rear-fanged).

Orbit The cavity in the skull containing the eye.

Osmosis The passage of soluble molecules from a less concentrated to a more concentrated solution.

Ossification Being converted to bone.

Osteoderm A bonelike plate or area beneath the scales in some reptiles.

Oviduct The canal which carries the ova from the ovary to the exterior via the cloaca.

Oviposition The act of laying or depositing eggs in specific sites.

Oviparous Egglaying.

Ovo-viviparous Describing an animal in which the eggs develop and hatch within the uterus of the female.

Palate The roof of the mouth.

Palatine The main bone plate in the palate.

Parietals A pair of bones forming the main part of the skull roof.

Parietal eye A vestigeal 'third eye', situated in the centre of the skull between the parietals.

Parthenogenetic Describing a method of reproduction in which the ova develop without fertilisation by the male gamete, producing offspring genetically identical to the parent.

Pathology The study of disease.

Pelagic Ocean dwelling (eg sea snakes).

Pelvic girdle The bony arch which supports the bones of the hind limbs in many vertebrates. Vestigeal in some lizards and snakes; absent in most snakes.

Permafrost Appertaining to areas of altitude or longitude where the ground remains permanently frozen.

Perspex Strong, highly transparent thermoplastic resin used to manufacture aquarium tanks. It is known as plexiglass in the USA.

Phalanges The bones of the digits.

Pharynx The part of the alimentary canal anterior to the oesophagus.

Phylogeny The history of the evolution of a species; normally used in classification.

Pleurodont With teeth set in a cavity on the inner side of the jawbone.

Polyphyodont With teeth which are replaced more than once.

Posterior Appertaining to the rear end of the body.

Prehensile Adapted for holding or grasping.

Premaxilla The teeth bearing bone at the front of the upper jaw.

Proteroglyphous Appertaining to snakes with canalised venom fangs at the front of the upper jaw and usually fixed (eg in the Elapidae).

Pulmonary artery The vessel supplying blood to the lung directly from the heart.

Pulmonary vein The vessel returning blood to the heart directly from the lung.

Quadrate The part of the upper jaw which forms the point of articulation with the lower jaw.

Radius One of a pair of bones in the forearm of tetrapods.

Rami The pair of structures forming the lower jaw or mandible (*sing.* ramus).

Rectilinear crawling A method of locomotion in snakes in which the reptile moves forward by complex movements of the ribs, muscles, and belly scales in a system of waves.

Reticulated Having a pattern of colour resembling a net.

Saliva The secretion of the salivary glands discharging into the buccal cavity. Contains enzymes and performs a lubricatory function. Venom glands in certain snakes are modifications of salivary glands.

Scapula The shoulder blade.

Scree Areas at the base of rocky slopes covered with rock fragments, ranging from boulder size to dust. Provides an ideal habitat for many reptile species.

Scrub Areas of land covered with one or more types of low vegetation.

Sexual dimorphism The condition in which the male and female of a species show obvious differences in colour or structure.

Solenoglyphous Appertaining to snakes with movable (hinged) canalised venom glands at the front of the upper jaw (eg Viperidae).

Spinal cord The main nerve of the body running from the brain to the tail through the neural canal.

Stapes A small bone connecting the tympanum (ear drum) and the inner ear.

Sternum A series of bones running through the central, ventral part of the thorax, to which the ribs are attached.

Stress A condition in animals in which psychological effects reduce resistance to disease. Applies particularly to newly captured, wild specimens.

Symphysis The joining of two bones with interlocking parts.

Taxonomy The study of the theory, rules and procedure of classification.

Temporal The area of the skull posterior to the orbits.

Terrestrial Mainly ground dwelling.

Thecodont Having teeth inserted in sockets.

Thermoreceptor A heat detecting organ (eg the 'pit' in pit vipers).

Thermoregulation The process used by ectotherms to maintain their preferred body temperature by moving in and out of areas of environmental warmth.

Trachea The canal which allows the passage of air to the lungs (*also*: wind pipe).

Tympanum The ear drum.

Ulna One of a pair of bones in the forelimb of tetrapods.

Uric acid A white, almost insoluble crystalline acid to which nitrogenous waste is converted by animals living in arid areas.

Vena cava A principal vein carrying blood to the heart from the posterior part of the body.

Vent The orifice of the cloaca.

Ventral Appertaining to the underside of the body.

Vestige The remains of an anatomical structure which has degenerated through evolution.

Viviparous Livebearers – those species which give birth to offspring in an advanced state of development.

Yolk A spherical mass of (usually) yellow nutritive fluid enclosed by the yolk sac and supportive of the developing embryo.
Zoogeography The study of the distribution of animals in relation to continents and climates.
Zoonoses Diseases which may be transmitted to man from animals. Very few reptilian diseases are pathogenic to man.

BIBLIOGRAPHY

It would be impracticable to list the many hundreds of references containing information on lizards, snakes and their captive care. For identification of species the reader should refer to some of the excellent field guides available, although some areas of the world remain to be comprehensively covered. The following is a list of books and papers which have been found to be useful in either general or specific aspects of herpetology. Some are outdated, but all remain interesting and informative.

Arnold, E.N. and Burton, J.A. 1978 *A Field Guide to the Reptiles and Amphibians of Europe*, Collins, London

Banks, C. 1980 *Keeping Reptiles and Amphibians as Pets*, Thomas Nelson, Melbourne

Behler, J.L. and King, F.W. 1979 *The Audubon Society Field Guide to North American Reptiles & Amphibians*, Alfred A. Knopf, New York

Bellairs, A. 1969 *The Life of Reptiles* (vols 1 & 2), Weidenfeld & Nicholson, London

Breen, J.F. 1974 *Encyclopaedia of Reptiles and Amphibians*, TFH Publications, New Jersey

Bruno, S. 1977 *Rettili d'Italia*, Giunti-Martello, Firenze (Florence)

Carr, A. 1963 *The Reptiles*, Life Nature Library, Time Inc, New York

Coborn, J. (Ed.) 1980 *European Herpetological Symposium Proceedings* (A collection of interesting conservation biased papers from various authors) Cotswold Wild Life Park, Burford, Oxon, UK

Coborn, J. 1985 *Beginner's Guide to Snakes*, Paradise Press, Queensland

Coborn, J. 1986 Snakes and Lizards in *UFAW Handbook on the Care and Management of Laboratory Animals*, Universities Federation for Animal Welfare, Potters Bar, Herts, UK

Cogger, H.G. 1979 *Reptiles and Amphibians of Australia*, A.H. & A.W. Reed, Sydney, Australia

Conant, R. 1975 *A Field Guide to the Reptiles and Amphibians of Eastern North America*, Houghtion Mifflin, Boston, USA

Cooper, J.E. and Jackson, O.F. 1981 *Diseases of the Reptilia* (vols 1 & 2) Academic Press, London

Ditmars, R.L. 1957 *Snakes of the World*, Macmillan, New York

Ditmars, R.L. 1960 *Reptiles of the World*, Macmillan, New York

Ferner, J.W. 1979 A Review of Marking Techniques for Amphibians and Reptiles, in *SSAR Herp. Circular No 9*, Athens, Ohio

Fitch, H.S. 1970 *Reproductive Cycles in Lizards and Snakes*, University of Kansas, Museum of Natural History

Fitzsimmons, V.F.M. 1970 *A Field Guide to the Snakes of Southern Africa*, Collins, London

Fretey, J. 1975 *Guide des Reptiles et Batraciens de France*, Hatier, Paris

Frye, F.L. 1973 *Husbandry, Medicine and Surgery in Captive Reptiles*, V.M. Publishing, Kansas

Gadow, H. 1901, reprint 1968 *Amphibia and Reptiles*, Macmillan, England (Reprint, Wheldon & Wesley, Codicote, England)

Goin, C.J. and Goin, O.B. 1971 *Introduction to Herpetology*, W.H. Freeman, New York

Honegger, R. 1979 Marking Reptiles and Amphibians for Future Recognition, in *International Zoo Yearbook*, Vol 19, pp 14–22 (Zoological Society of London)

Huff, T.A. 1977 Caging and Feeding Techniques Employed at the Reptile Breeding Foundation, *Proceedings of the Second Annual Symposium on Captive Propagation and Husbandry*, pp 15–20, Thurmont, Md. USA

Jackson, O.F. 1976 Reptiles, in *A Manual of the Care and Treatment of Children's and Exotic Pets*, BSAVA Publications, London

Jahn, J. 1963 *Kleine Terrarienkunde*, Albrecht Philler Verlag, Minden, Germany

Kauffeld, C. 1969 *Snakes: The Keeper and the Kept*, Doubleday, New York

Klauber, L.M. 1956 *Rattlesnakes*, University of California Press, Berkeley

Klingelhoffer, W. and Scherpner, C.H.R. 1955–59 *Terrarienkunde* (vols 1–4) Alfred Kernen Verlag, Stuttgart

Leutscher, A. and Dakeyne, H. 1952 *Vivarium Life*, Cleaver Hume Press, London

Loveridge, A. 1945 *Reptiles of the Pacific World*, Macmillan, New York

Mattison, C. 1982 *The Care of Reptiles and Amphibians in Captivity*, Blandford Press, Poole, Dorset, UK

Minton, S.A. and Minton, M.R. 1971 *Venomous Reptiles*, George Allen & Unwin, London

Murphy, J.B. and Collins, J.T. (Eds) 1980 *Reproductive Biology and Diseases of Captive Reptiles*, Society for the Study of Reptiles and Amphibians, USA

Nietzke, G. 1969–72 *Die Terrarientiere* (vols 1 & 2), Eugen Ulmer Verlag, Stuttgart

Phelps, T. 1981 *Poisonous Snakes*, Blandford Press, Poole, Dorset, UK

Pitman, C.R.S. 1974 *A Guide to the Snakes of Uganda*, (Reprint,) Wheldon & Wesley, Codicote, England

Riches, R.J. 1976 *Breeding Snakes in Captivity*, Palmetto Publishing, Florida

Robb, J. 1980 *New Zealand Amphibians and Reptiles*, Collins, Auckland

Stebbins, R.C.A. 1966 *A Field Guide to Western Reptiles and Amphibians*, Houghton Mifflin, Boston, USA

Stettler, P.H. 1978 *Handbuch der Terrarienkunde*, Fränck'sche Verlagshandlung, W. Keller u., Stuttgart

Townson, S., Millichamp, N.J., Lucas, D.G.D. and Millwood, A.J. (Eds) 1980 *The Care and Breeding of Captive Reptiles*, British Herpetological Society, London

Webb, J.E., Wallwork, J.A. and Elgood, J.H. 1978 *Guide to Living Reptiles*, Macmillan, London and Basingstoke

INDEX

INDEX OF SCIENTIFIC NAMES

GENERAL INDEX